Only the Dance
Essays on Time
and Memory

Only the Dance

Essays on Time and Memory
by Judith Kitchen

UNIVERSITY OF SOUTH CAROLINA PRESS

Published in Columbia, South Carolina, by the
University of South Carolina Press

Manufactured in the United States of America

Library of Congress Cataloging-in-Publication Data

Kitchen, Judith.
    Only the dance : essays on time and memory / Judith Kitchen
      p.   cm.
    Includes bibliographical references.
    Contents: Things of this life—Floral clock, Edinburgh, August 2—
  Hide-and-go-seek—Culloden, August 6—Robert Jimmy Allen—"Over
  the sea to Skye," August 9—Research—York Minster, August 10—
  Midge—North Yorkshire, August 11—Picnic at paradise—Greenhill
  Gate, August 12—Not less because: ways of looking at Wallace
  Stevens, Haworth, August 13—Ten stories—White roads: the
  landscapes of Leslie Norris, Wales, August 15—Lists of Salcombe,
  August 17—Transitional—Hardy's cottage, August 19—Songs to
  undo the spring—Only the dance.
    ISBN 1–57003–022–7
    I. Title.
  PS3561.I845O55 1994
  813'.54—dc20   94–18681
                                                                CIP

In memory of:

my mother,
Lillian Pendell Randels
(1907–1980)

my grandfather,
George B. Randels
(1876–1942)

my aunt,
Margaret Randels Warner
(1915–1972)

my uncle,
William C. Randels
(1909–1992)

Contents

Acknowledgments

Some of these essays appeared in the following magazines: "Hide-and-Go Seek" and "Ten Stories" in *The Georgia Review*; "Lists" in *The Laurel Review*; "Midge" and "Robert Jimmy Allen" in *River City*; "Not Less Because" in *The Wallace Stevens Journal* and "Haworth" in *Creative Nonfiction*. "Research" is reprinted from *Prairie Schooner* by permission of the University of Nebraska Press, copyright 1991 University of Nebraska Press. "Songs to Undo the Spring" originally appeared in the Spring 1993 issue of *The Gettysburg Review* and "Picnic at Paradise" appeared in the Summer 1994 issue of *The Gettysburg Review*.

"White Roads: The Landscape of Leslie Norris" was published in *An Open World: Essays on Leslie Norris*, ed. Eugene England and Peter Makuck (Columbia, SC: Camden House, Inc., 1993). "Robert Jimmy Allen" is included in *Where We Stand: Women Poets on Literary Tradition*, ed. Sharon Bryan (New York: W. W. Norton, 1993). In addition, "Hide-and-Go-Seek" was awarded a 1990 Pushcart Prize; "Hide-and-Go-Seek" and "Research" were each listed as notable essays in *Best American Essays*, 1990 and 1992.

I would like to express gratitude for a National Endowment for the Arts Fellowship which enabled me to write and travel to the United Kingdom. I would also like to thank all of you who gave me sound advice along with your encouragement—my writing group (Mary Paumier Jones, Jane Schuster, Gwen Nelson, Jim DeCamp, Carol Wisner, Gail Bouk, Gail Gilberg, Anne Day, Carol Burelbach, Larry Sill, Jeannette Delamoir), those friends who have supported this project through the years, Steve Heller, Nancy Simpson, Linda Allardt, Bruce Bennett Stanley, W. Lindberg, my editors, Warren Slesinger and Margaret V. Hill whose support has been invaluable, and my family, Bob, George, Matthew, Robin, William, Elizabeth, and, as always, Stan.

Only the Dance
Essays on Time
and Memory

The present rips apart and
joins together again; it begins;
it is beginning itself. It has a past,
but in the form of remembrance.
It has a history, but it is not history.

—Emmanuel Levinas, *Time and the Other*

Things of This Life

Consider the child idly browsing in the curio shop. She's been on vacation in the Adirondacks, and her family has (over the past week) canoed the width of the lake and up a small, meandering river to where the beaver dams have made passage impossible; found a stable and spent an afternoon on horseback; cooked pancakes and hot dogs and beef stew over a campfire; and spent each evening lying stretched on their backs on a canvas tarp, hoping to catch sight of the meteor showers as the darkness deepens. So why, as she sifts through boxes of fake arrowheads made into key chains, passes down the long rows of rubber tomahawks, dyed rabbits' feet, salt shakers with the words "Indian Lake" painted in gold, beaded moccasins made of what could only in the imagination be called leather, is she happier than any time during the past week?

The child could spend hours like this, touching and putting back, lifting, holding, choosing. Her father cannot understand it. Her brother has chosen quickly, paid, and left to wrestle with his friend in the gravel parking lot. She can hear their syncopated scuffling. Her mother shares a bit of her desire, but is a practical woman and can already see that nothing here will last. So the child feels guilty as well as drawn, and she can't make up her mind. "Ten more minutes," says her father, "that's all." And so she chooses, reluctantly letting go of the alternate dreams. She picks a round box made of bark, she thinks, decorated with porcupine quills. It smells like sweet grass, like countryside. She counts out her quarters and nickels and emerges, squinting, with her purchase. "What are you going to do with that?" her brother asks, and she realizes that she doesn't know. "It feels nice," she says.

Now consider the woman who was that child. Today she wakes up in her untidy bedroom with sunlight slanting through the panes where she has recently adjusted the blinds. Outside, there is snow and for some reason that makes the sunlight brighter, sadder. There has been too much snow this winter and she is tired of it, tired of stepping out of the passenger seat of the car into a wall of snow that filters into her shoes, tired of keeping the porch steps swept for the mailman, tired of the way everyone talks about nothing but weather. She's tired of driving home on Tuesday nights with the wind in her face and the thin snakes of snow rippling fastforward out in front on the asphalt. She's tired of how the flakes flare briefly in the headlights, and how she can't somehow see beyond them into the receding dark. She's almost tired of wondering why the tracks—footprints in the yard, snowmobile in the field—are whiter than the surrounding expanse of snow so that you see them as a trail of pure light. Or why the blue evening, cold at the edges, makes the houselights seem so lonely. So this morning she stirs and then closes her eyes to the glare, turns toward the wall.

Consider what she sees there, against the grey wall of her bedroom, between the closet and the doorway into the study. For a moment, she's a child again, everything familiar. The dresser is squat, waist-high, with three drawers. Dark walnut, with carved handles. When she was little, this dresser was in the dining room, filled with carefully ironed linen tablecloths, napkins, the flowered glass place tags that her mother never used because they were too nice. In its new location, there is a drawer for sweaters, one for scarves, and the top drawer holds gifts she's saving for some occasion or another. At the moment it has a blue ceramic soap dish, a writing pad, three books, a set of woven coasters, two tea towels, a pot holder, a tape of southern fiddle music. She has no one in mind for any of these items.

On top of the dresser—it seems (to her eye) pleasantly crowded—there is a handcrafted jack-in-the-box whose insides, which have "popped," reveal themselves as a green felt frog with a black velvet cape lined in red satin. He has a gold monocle on one eye. There is also a vase with flowers, just beginning to wilt. (She'd been sick and he'd brought them.) That's the only thing that isn't usually there. The other items include a shallow bowl with fluted edges which might, anywhere else, be called gaudy. The interior is pink, and the outside is covered with painted flowers in deep blue, yellow, white, with orange centers. She keeps necklaces in it—including the string of wooden beads her son made for her when he was nine. There are two painted baskets, one for bracelets and one for pins. And a ceramic mug (whose handle fell off so neatly it looks like a vase) where she keeps loose quarters and dimes. Two painted wooden tops seem never to have found another place to call their own, and there's a lacquered box—what we now call Chinese red—which is really a deep-throated rust, with a gold tree spreading across its cover. And—again from her childhood—a tiny porcelain piano. When she lifts its lid, inside is curled a pair of earrings she could not bear not to own, waiting for the day she might have the courage to pierce her ears.

Sometimes, in the mirror, she holds them up to her face. She becomes someone she does not quite recognize. She wants to drive quickly to the mall and ask to have it done before she can change her mind. It can't be all that painful. But, she wonders, would a woman in those earrings ever throw back her head and

3

laugh long and loud? Would she cry, huge gulping sobs? She tosses her head to watch the effect. Who would she be with those elegant earrings elongating her face, holding her to their standards of decorum?

Sometimes she does not want to get out of bed. Beyond this room there are others, each of them holding the things with which she has surrounded herself, the tiny objects her hands have sampled and selected. If she listed them to herself, it would take hours. If she were to move, how would she choose among them? What is the relative value of the glass paperweight, the paper fan, the cracked blue tile from Belgium? Besides, don't these things belong together, especially now that they have grown used to each other, used to being her objects of desire? Don't they welcome the next item as she finds it? Don't they all move over, make room, accommodate? Don't they take on new lustre in its presence? Don't they preen and shine?

So, as she stirs, turns, opens her left eye, lets it rest on the green frog, run itself over the soft body, burrowing for texture and light, she feels safe for a moment, lost once more in the long dusty rows of the shop, fingering and fingering her way toward the things of this life. Because this life, as she knows it, is alien still. Even after five years, it doesn't quite feel like her life—the one she knew how to live. She has surrounded herself with her things to remind her that she is really here, in this house, with this man. "This is your life now," they tell her, since her dreams still haven't caught up and (as often as not) she inhabits other spaces in the depth of the night. Her old life closes in with its shapeless certainties as she crosses its threshhold.

In the clean, uncritical light of morning, the room leaps to life and she rises famished. She wants bacon and eggs on a green Fiestaware plate—and whole wheat toast with Scottish marmalade. If there were tomatoes in the refrigerator, she'd want a grilled tomato, carefully cut into two halves, each with a serrated edge, like her fluted bowl. But she'll settle for mushrooms, sautéed with butter and garlic. Or an orange, peeled and quartered, the way they serve dessert in the Japanese restaurant. With a little toothpick.

Here's what she'd tell you: her hands know beauty when they feel it. Oh, there are drawings on the walls—a hunting print from Wales, old maps—but those are merely decoration. She wants to lift and savor, to settle something into place. She wishes every day were Christmas and she could bring out her wooden angel, the rope horse from Brazil, the origami swan, making this life dance like her tree, a tangle of old and new, a confusion of time and place all held together by one hand—hers.

Think of it: she doesn't know who she is or where she belongs. She buys the Mexican salad bowl and the two wooden spoons and places them in the middle of the table so she'll know she should be here. Look around. No one else would put her grandmother's little trunk next to the wicker picnic basket. If she closes her eyes, she can see her grandmother's proper handwriting, purled on the edges of envelopes, careful and precise. Mayme, who never finished eighth grade after her mother died and she had to take care of her brothers and sisters, who had to work hard on the farm but who knew how to spell and who kept every letter she ever received. Even the ones with the wobbly scrawl that said *Dear Grandma Pendell, Thank you for the present. I wish we could see you soon. I am already seven. Love.* Here's the way it happened: the train's shrill whistle, crescendo, then a bright hole in the dark and the thunder of steam. Mayme would step onto the platform wearing a dark purple coat, her black braids wound tightly around her head. Her skin was too soft and wrinkly. When you kissed her cheek, it wobbled, and you wished you didn't have to do that. What you really wished was that you could go to her place in Michigan to visit your cousins' farm and ride in the back of the wagon and see the baby pigs. And you wished you could run off by yourself in the meadow and lie back in the grass and see, up close (so close your own eye might be a telescope), the buttercups on their spindly stems above you. Shards of sunlight. And the sky behind them blue forever. The only sound would be wind and you'd know it was wind even though it was only a tickle. It was the kind of quiet that seemed as if something had been taken away. Today, she'd call it a hush. Meaning that sound had receded. Meaning an absence that fills itself up with a word.

Think of her now, beginning her day. She was that child. How can she go on, wanting like this, for the rest of her life? How can she bear to think of next week, next month when she will meet friends she hasn't seen for too long? It's too late to lose twenty pounds or to grow her fingernails. Who will she be? There's not even time to pierce her ears and enter the room as a new and different woman. She will have to attend the ball as herself. She will need to find herself quickly. She will need to sort through so many boxes, untie so many ribbons. At the very least, she will need to buy a new blouse in a fabric that begs to be fondled. She wants to be touched. She wants to become the very thing they cannot do without.

Floral Clock

Edinburgh, August 2

West Princes Street Gardens has the first ever
Floral Clock which was constructed in 1904.
                              —Frommer's *Scotland*

Memory is trickery. For thirty years this clock was large. It covered an entire hillside of the Princes Street Gardens, 20,000 annuals all tended by a full-time gardener. Now I see that it's really quite small, tucked away between the stone steps and the railing. We stare as we climb, stopping to admire the design, the basic miracle that it works at all—plants carefully selected so one hand slides easily over the other as they point to each perfectly cultivated Roman numeral on the hill. Every quarter hour is punctuated by a hidden cuckoo. We wait for the call.

I'm back in the city in which I first fell in love. In love first of all *with* the city—with streetlights on wet cobblestones, dark winter evenings, a slow, damp cold, and whatever it was that could make me warm. Time, then, was a ride on the top of a double-decker bus. It was hanging on to the pole at the foot of the stairs, waiting for our corner, jumping off. It knocked at the door and we opened it. We raced up the down escalator. At the zoo, the

7

mynah bird asked, "Where's Charlie? Where's the pretty boy?"

Time, now, is a feathery thing. It flees in the dark, rounding the corner as I appear. Like sunlight, there's never enough. The world spins and we will have to get off. We all have to get off.

I go back to the row of stone houses and show my new husband the second-floor flat I called home. I feel neither nostalgia nor pain. Nothing.

And yet, when I left that marriage, I felt more guilt than rancor. There's a kind of grief that only the leavers know. Don't expect sympathy. That's for those who are left. We all know what they're going through—if only in imagination. The grief of the leaver is a clock without hands.

Thirty years later the house is still the same. I tell Stan how birds pecked the foil on the bottles of milk we kept on the sill. How we put a penny over the cap to fool the birds. The window's the same, but I've moved on. Now I'm here with someone new. He presses the shutter to capture where I used to live. Dead house of a dead marriage. Shuttered stone.

In Stan's eyes, the city comes to life. Summer day, tea and scones, the winding river Leith. We wind our way through separate pasts. "Where's Charlie? Where's the pretty boy?" Where are we now, the two who were here? And where are the others? Christina? Stephen? Neil? The past wrapped in names, tied in a tidy pink ribbon. Hold them, like love letters, so they don't disappear. So nothing goes wrong. No one shows up at the door in bell-bottomed trousers and a mind hazy on drugs. No one loses her breast. No one dies. *Christina, hold on.*

Tomorrow we will leave for the north. We search for the cuckoo—sound out of sight. Thirty years smaller, we wait for the call.

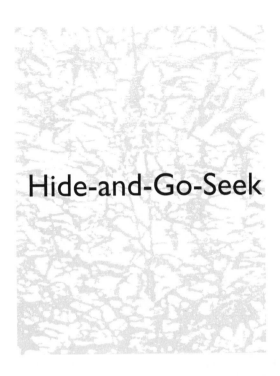

Hide-and-Go-Seek

I am sitting on the deck of a house in Maine, overlooking the Atlantic Ocean. Below me, lobster boats are making their daily rounds—sputter of engine, flutter of gulls. It is supposed to be beautiful and, I guess, you could say it is. *I* could say it is. But I am bored. I want something else, though I'm not sure what. Last year was the same. I ran out of books to read and then I was bored—ornery bored. The nearest bookstore is sixty-eight miles southwest on Route 1, plus the seven miles over narrow roads to reach Route 1, and the mile and a half of ruts from the house to paved road.

So I bought puzzles at a local auction, 1,500-piece puzzles spread out on the table—the kind where you have to make the distinction between the thing and the shadow of the thing. Believe me, I know every nook and cranny of the Grand Canyon at sunset, every shimmering reflection of autumn leaves in a New Hampshire stream. But I was still bored. I spent time lying nude on the deck, stretched out in the sun with my mind as blank as I could make it. Little red swirls in front of the eyes, pinpoints of heat. Nothing else. But my body resisted. I went home more red than brown, more white than red, a patchwork of attempts to be what I am not.

This year is different. I came armed with a boxful of books, something for every mood. *Love in the Time of Cholera. The Songlines.* Vivian Gornick's memoirs of life with her mother. Mystery. Poetry. Fiction. Today I brought my coffee out to the deck, along with Tim O'Brien's *The Nuclear Age.* The steam from my cup rises, becomes a part of the fog burning off in the late morning sun. The open book pulls me into its pages. Catches me off guard:

> *"Like hide-and-go-seek—the future curves toward the past then folds back again, seamlessly, always expressing itself in the present tense."*

I'm sure Tim O'Brien only wanted to repeat a line that sounded good. That gave him easy access to his next thought. That allowed him to move from where he was to where he wanted to be. Even so . . .

. . . *the future curves* and I am ten. It is late July, early August, the height of summer boredom. The whole neighborhood is waiting for something to happen. We spent the last days of June riding our bicycles up and down maple-covered streets, poking sticks into the muddy, overfull banks of the Cohocton, free from school and from parents, free to make the village our own. And July brought a smattering of one-week vacations—families stuffed into cars filled with camping gear, off to the Adirondacks—mosquitoes, canoe trips, outdoor toilets, those flimsy moccasins I bought every year hoping they might last. And then home to baseball games on the back lot, six or seven to a team, short tempers, the inevitable cheating, the heated shouts of "out" "no, *safe*" "no, *out*" until we all quit in disgust. By this point in the summer I have picked quart upon quart of raspberries, carefully settled the slatted boxes into the bed of the red wagon, bribed my brother to knock on the doors, and sold them up and down the hillside. I've spent some of my earnings at Tombasco's fruit stand, a popsicle a day while the season lasts. I've eaten every flavor Basco has to sell. I've stood on his oiled wood floors, dripping sticky purple juice, watching the flies circle and circle the tomatoes and cucumbers, finally favoring the peaches and watermelons and the temptations of scent. I've grown sick of popsicles that never deliver what they promise, tucked in tantalizing rows in Basco's deep freezer. I've grown heartily sick of summer, and there is still a month to go.

A month of baby games: tag, kick-the-can, kick-the-can-in-the-dark. A dozen variations on hide-and-go-seek. "Draw a circle on the old man's back. Here's two eyes, and a mouth. Who will put the nose?" The quick stab of forefinger in the back. The whirling about to see if someone is still moving. The smug look on everyone's face. The guessing. "Donna." No, you're wrong. And the one who did it—Billy or Jimmy or George or Steve or Marilyn—giving you the penance: "Crawl on your hands and knees to Joel Sundquist's front steps, saying 'I love Joel' at each crack in the sidewalk, then get up and walk backwards to the tree, count to fifty, then you can look." Variations on humiliation.

. . . toward the past. It is the summer they built the Catholic church in town. Until now, ours has been a three-church town. A walk up Hamilton and there is the Presbyterian church, all cool brick and music and stained glass, a steeple that reaches for the sky. Turn the corner and it's Methodist, white painted wood, a rectangle, solid and simple. Simply there. And then on Water Street, facing the dike, the Baptist church—grey concrete, a sort of fake stone. It has two steeples, one shorter than the other, giving it the lopsided look of a man limping. That's what this town is like. Protestant to the hilt, but regular. Nothing fancy like Episcopal or Lutheran. Nothing too plain, like the Quakers. Which is why, during the summer months when people don't go to services so often, the three churches take turns holding them. For three months everyone is the same, then they break apart

again into what they have always been because their mothers and fathers were before them. Catholics? Sure, they're here, but they've always gone over to the Saints—St. Joseph's in the next town, or St. Vincent's three miles further, because it has a school.

The bulldozer pulls up at the vacant lot on the corner of our street, stopping next to the sign that has been there all summer, meaningless: *Our Lady of the Immaculate Conception.* Suddenly, at the end of the summer, there is activity, something to watch, something to *do.* By evening there is a deep hole on the corner lot, and piles of dirt waiting for us to run up and down, in and out, in the long hours after dinner. The next day the dirt is trucked away and the hole is so huge and deep that our parents are telling us to stay away from it.

By the end of the week, the men have lined the hole with cinder blocks and poured concrete. By the beginning of the next, they are erecting cinder-block walls within the hole, an open maze of rooms with spaces left for doorways, an underground life still open to the sky. The men place boards across these spaces so they will not have to walk around. Three, four, then six, seven feet from the bottom—the men crisscross the maze of cinder blocks, trowels in hand, smoothing and fitting. Then, miraculously, they stop work. They must be waiting for something— plywood or bricks.

For four days the maze is ours. By day we survey it, memorizing where the boards are placed, imagining our way across the planks, twisting and turning in a million intricate moves. In the thin evening light, we play the game we have invented: hide-and-go-seek-in-the-dark. We play it over the church cellar—those are the rules. We inch our way out onto the planks and move, foot by foot, to the next wall. We work our way out to the center, balanced precariously high over concrete. A fall could be fatal, or at least could put a stop to the game, so we are careful. Our parents do not know where we are—only that we are playing again, that we do not seem so bored, that they have another hour of peace before they must call us in for bed. They do not know that we are testing our bodies against our minds. That what is at stake is memory. That the one who knows best where each board is placed is the one who will win.

I am ten. I inch myself out onto the plank, pick up speed, scurry to the outside wall, veer left, hop out onto the next board, over the space left for a doorway, out and over the whole of the church, around and around, twist and turn, hardly groping in the dark, my feet full of instinct, my mind as alert as it will ever be. I hop over the last obstacle, reach solid ground, sprint for the big tree in front of Mrs. Hale's house, "*homefree*" and I'm first, I'm home safe.

. . . folds back again. But in the present I am sitting on the deck of a house in Maine, overlooking the Atlantic Ocean. Below me . . . I am bored. I am ten. But that is the past in the present, such intense boredom that it dares the mind to outflank the body. Is it the past curving toward the future I am sensing, or is it the present curving toward the past? What do I make of this memory—as real to me here, stretched out in sunlight, as it was then in the first hush of evening in the waning days of my last childish summer? Surely the past holds out something to the future as the loop shortens and folds. The present is tangential, touching only at this point, the here, the now. How can I dare to admit to being bored? How can the present count for nothing, when this is all I have? Each moment finite. Half behind me, half stretching so interminably ahead.

Four days was all we had. After that, the bricks arrived, and the two-by-fours, and the hardwood and stained glass, so that by October there was an edifice where before there had been nothing. And by November we were not even surprised to see it, hardly remembered the vacant lot or the summer evenings or the games. We were eleven. We were busy belonging. We wore saddle shoes. We liked Ike. We were caught up in school, and something more. Boys. Not Billy or Steve or Gordie—not neighborhood boys. No, this was different.

I sat on one side of Mrs. Harrison's sixth grade and looked across the room to where John LeBarron pretended not to notice any of us. I thought about his dark hair, and the way he moved, and the mystery he brought with him down from the hills, riding the bus miles into town. In art class, we made identification bracelets. Narrow for girls, with roses engraved over our names. Wider for boys, with a sports motif. Each day a new girl would show up with a boy's bracelet on her wrist. I wanted John LeBarron's bracelet—more than I wanted John LeBarron. What would I say to *him?* I wanted that bracelet more than anything in the world. And the world had changed. Looped. I felt my life ahead of me, a strand of desire, stretched thin and thinner, and there, always there, waiting, the present tense about to pounce.

Sputter of engines. The lobster boat turns sharply, homing in on the buoys. A tug and the trap seems to lift itself into the boat. Gulls swarm. A pause, engines almost off, as the trap is inspected, the lobster removed and measured, the trap baited and then, in a quick motion, it soars free of the boat, drops seaward. One flick of the wrist and the gulls go crazy, scattering over the sea, scavenging. Sputter of engines, the boat turns again, sets its sights, churns toward a small painted dot in the sea.

. . . *present tense*. Again and again, and I am familiar with the boat's pattern as though I had known it all my life. But I haven't. I have known it for precisely one year—from last summer to this. And yet the knowledge feels as solid as the knowledge of the Perseids, those showers of shooting stars I have watched each summer since I was eight. Or the knowledge of how to ice skate, one foot gliding out with such assurance, waiting for the other to pick up the cadence, begin its own thrust and glide, the two feet synchronized, out and over the ice, like wind. Or the knowledge of desire, which was swimming below my summer boredom waiting to surface in the guise of John LeBarron's surly indifference, and swims now, in circles, asserting itself.

I am fourteen and it's there in earnest. High school is a sea of desire. I save my reading for home, for the quiet warmth of the hot air registers and the cool privacy of thought. High school is where we test and retest our abilities to attract. No one is better at this than Mary Agnes, my new best friend. She came this year, from St. Vincent's, and she has set the school on fire. She's short and dark and cute as a button, has been all her life. She knows how to use it—flash of black eyes, wrinkle of nose, flick of the skirt. She's a cheerleader, too, and seems to lead cheers all day long—everything needs to be whipped up to match her enthusiasm. To *hold* it. It's fun to swim along in her wake. Everything is new.

First cigarette. We're standing in October leaves behind Mary Agnes's kitchen window. The stale taste, the aroma of fall, the crunch of leaves underfoot, it's all one and the same. It's the glow of four cigarettes in the dark, pinpoints of light, flickering fireflies of evidence. And it's the furious flurry, the scuttle, the stamping of feet on dropped butts as the headlights swing into the driveway and her parents are home. It's the innocent way we all stand, pulling our identical blue and white corduroy jackets around us, laughing, practicing cheers as though that were our passion and we had been working through dusk. "One, two, three, four, who are we for?" We are for excitement. For something new. Something that will help the boredom of routine lives in a small town. Something akin to desire.

What do we know of desire? We know only what it is to want to be wanted. And we want to be wanted in the worst way, by the right kind of boys—the ones who will make other girls jealous. We want basketball stars, tall and smooth, the ball swooshing through the net without touching the rim. We want the good-looking boys, the ones who know they're cute. We want the older boys in the back of the room—we don't care if they've been held back. We aren't interested in their minds. We want the bored expressions on their faces. We want to feel our hearts beat as they pull us toward them, pull our faces deep into the front of their leather jackets, we want to smell hair oil and something sharper, more urgent. We want to have them kiss us with hard, angry lips. We want to feel our cheeks redden on the sandpaper of their cheeks. We want the stab of fear as they fumble for our breasts, pushing us back roughly against the pine trees. We want to be wanted. We take pains. We match skirts and sweaters, we pincurl our hair, we learn the new dances, the words to the songs.

We watch Beth Collins running around the block. Around and around, every night she runs and runs, exhausted. What is she doing? After four or five nights we figure it out. She is pregnant. She is trying to run her baby out of her body. We figure it out because, to us, it is clear. Close to us. To adults, it is not so clear. We watch for two more nights, holding our breath, feeling every inch of our bodies, how they fold inside themselves, secret and scared. By day, Beth drags herself through school. There are circles under her eyes, she looks bloated and sad and slightly desperate. What should we do? Mary Agnes has no doubts. She dials the Collinses' number, puts a handkerchief over the phone, and in a deep voice says, "Tell Beth it won't work." Then we watch as Mrs. Collins throws open her backdoor, glances toward our window as though she almost suspects, walks slowly down to the sidewalk to wait for Beth to turn the corner. Two weeks later Beth is "visiting her aunt in Indiana" for the rest of the year. We are awed. Mary Agnes can get away with anything.

It's so real. I can see Beth running in her old white sweatshirt, her red hair weaving behind, her ponytail brushing first one shoulder then the other. I can hear Mary Agnes lower her voice and my own quickened heartbeat. What do I make of a past more real than the present? When it comes unbidden, like desire? What does it want? I have this sunlight stretching over waves, waves of heated air, my body stretched on the deck, my mind as clear and sharp as ever, ready for the future. But the future only curves *toward* and then folds *back*, not really touching. I am left with the future I am making now. How boring. A future of sitting in the sun over the Atlantic, remembering. My own inaction. My body's tense waiting. This does not make a memory, I'm almost certain of that. It will be just one of those ordinary days that recede and fade, that become the compost pile of a life. The hidden residue on which others grow. Unless something happens.

What usually happens, for me, is other people. They shape, through distraction. For instance, the man I am with is reading Virginia Woolf. Soon he will come out on the deck and read me a passage that interests him. I will have to admit to myself that I am not very interested in that passage—or any other. That I am bored by Virginia Woolf. It has taken years of composting to be able to say that. A woman is supposed to like Virginia Woolf. A woman is supposed to understand her feminine sensibility. But that's the problem, that's *why* she bores me. Women are not interested in other women. They are interested in men. And in themselves. Virginia Woolf is too much like me to interest me. I feel as though I could see things her way—*do* see things her way. Her thoughts *occur* to me.

He likes Virginia Woolf. She opens doors for him, puts a sentence together that twists and turns and takes him with her. I get tired of her incessant seeing, her ever-present *now* with its tidy observations. I get tired of Virginia the way I get tired of another woman on the phone when I am listening just to be polite, waiting for my turn to tell what's on my mind. I never feel that way with a man on the phone. I'm waiting for that little spark that says this conversation has undertone, and undertow. My mind on alert.

In the end, I must come to the disturbing conclusion that I am interested only in *my* life. I wish that I felt more disturbed about this than I do, that it sent me into a novelist's version of panic—no more characters to people my deepest dreams. But I am satisfied with the characters who come, at random, into my life, and with wondering just what they mean, what they have meant, what they are about to mean in the drama that is mine and mine alone. I am satisfied to play this game of hide-and-go-seek. It's only the present that tugs at the body, saying "Get up. Get going. Make something of this day."

Make something. Make a phone call. Do. Act. Is memory made up of verbs? Perhaps. Verbs and adjectives. With the hindsight of memory, we paint in color and shape. Similes. At the time, we live only the moment, unaware of comparison, or the hint of connection. In memory we piece things together, give them the "that must be why" or the "now I can see" that sews up the seam of a life. Tim O'Brien is wrong. Life is not seamless. It's a myriad of seams, a patchwork quilt. But the seamstress is as quick and as accurate as my grandmother Randels, who pieced together little octagons of colored cloth, flower after calico flower. They took shape in her fingers, a field full of wildflowers spreading over the bed, quilt after quilt, until her death left a boxful of unfinished flowers, a lifetime of seams invisible to the unpracticed eye.

I am fifteen. The phone rings and it is Mary Agnes. "Come on over. Don't tell anyone." That's all she says. It's nine o'clock and I don't see how my parents are going to understand the necessity of going out. But I tell them Mary Agnes is locked out of her house and I'm going to help her get the cellar window open, and then, just for good measure, that we're going to the diner for a hamburger because she hasn't had any dinner. Fine, they say. They seem to believe whatever I tell them. I almost believe she *is* locked out as I run the three blocks to her house. There she is, standing with a set of keys in her hands, pacing the driveway. I almost say "You found them" before I remember.

"Come on. Get in." Her father's white Cadillac is parked in front of the garage. "Get in." The question goes underground, but it is still there. "They're out of town. Won't be back till midnight." But we are fifteen and we haven't taken driver's training and we don't even have a permit, let alone a license. We don't know how to drive.

Or rather, *I* don't know how to drive. What Mary Agnes knows never ceases to amaze me. She slowly backs the car up, turns it around, noses it out onto the street, heading confidently out of town, stopping at each sign as though she had done it for years. Sitting next to her, in the dark plush of the passenger seat, I feel almost as safe as with my father. I don't relax, but I don't feel quite so nervous either. She heads for the back roads of the country around Gang Mills. The lights pry open the darkness, letting us own a small stretch of road. Up and down the dirt roads, dust spewing behind us, faster and faster—we begin to laugh, I stick my feet out the window, we wave as we streak past the mailboxes giving them at least four inches to spare. This is the limit of our world. We piece each stretch of the road to the next. We are the present—this motion, this exhilaration. A moving present, winding through the landscape.

At ten-thirty I am home. By eleven I'm asleep. The next morning Mary Agnes describes what I missed—how she went out again, driving the Cadillac up Rand Street where the railroad shunt cuts a lane of its own toward the factory. Straddling the rails, eighty miles an hour, right in town! I am not quite so taken with all of this as I pretend to be. I don't want to be left out, but I don't want to die. I want to come close, but veer off at the last minute. I'm not convinced Mary Agnes knows when to veer.

She's moving beyond us and we can feel it. She's finding new things to do—older, more experienced boys. I like it best when it feels familiar. Friday night, the diner after the basketball game, hamburgers and cokes. "Father Rogers would want me to eat this since it's already been ordered." Father Rogers is so understanding of her desires. I want a Father Rogers who knows what's best for me. I like Friday nights, all of us squeezed into a booth, Scott Dalrymple and his friends teasing, stealing our hats or mittens. But I can see it in her eyes. Boring. They glance over the formica table, the red vinyl benches, the confusion of teenagers, and they go distant. Darker. And suddenly it looks so ordinary, so hopelessly commonplace.

Yesterday I picked blueberries and made my own pie. Fields of wild blueberries, the sun on my back. Blueberries staining my fingers and the promise of pie. The sun like a compress. A bowl full of berries and a future tied to the present—no seams. And today I lie on the deck with the sure taste of the pie in my mouth— the taste of yesterday. No watch. No glasses. My body alive to the present. I close my eyes. The sound of sunlight is a deep rumble and intermittent churning of engines. Time is an ocean breeze that drops, suddenly, leaving a gap in the day. Whatever I am doing now won't count in that future. I am not here. I am alive in the greens and blues of the past. For this minute, or hour, there is no tense. I am on the underside of the quilt, moving with the thread that pulls it all together.

Desire does not rise as often in a life as we like to think it does. We spend our time waiting for it to reach out to us, wanting to be wanted. Real desire is the other side of that. It simply wants. It fastens itself on its object, unaware of self. It doesn't last—except in memory, where it rises again and again without warning. Always a surprise, always powerful.

I have five images of desire—only five times that *really* stand out. Count them on one hand. Maybe this is different for men, but I doubt it. I don't mean fleeting attractions. I mean the kind of desire that takes over and immobilizes. Five images that represent the spaces in my life where the focus is outward. Images. Held in the mind. Forever. Or revised, for common consumption. Real moments that stand for a succession of events or feelings. Real moments, although sometimes they happen only in the imagination.

First, nineteen, almost twenty, I turn a corner and can't go back. All night I wanted to be wanted, and then, on a hill in the Bronx, traffic making a red-and-yellow snake of lights below, I only want. What does he look like? He is twenty. Dark eyes, sardonic smile. Of course it can't work. His parents are threatening to cover the mirrors and say the prayers for the dead. So he dies, instead, for me. He will always be twenty, standing on a hill. Below him the weaving string of lights moves toward infinity.

Then I am dancing in the basement of St. Columba's Church in Edinburgh, Scotland. A young man with long curly hair is rushing down the stairs, rushing so fast he tumbles the last few, a blur of color and movement that I will interpret as love, and I am married and I speak in the first person plural and soon there is one son and then another and I rush on into a life my mother would surely approve. I am dancing in the basement of a church and there is nothing but color and motion, and perhaps some distant music.

There is one moment so fleeting I hardly know it was there, but I have evidence. A photograph. Not of him, but of me. A photograph I hardly recognize as myself, so unlike what I see in

20

the mirror. But the mirror wants to be wanted, aids and abets. In the photograph, I am open to his lens: a woman with hair to her shoulders, wearing white, holding a flower. Caught in the act.

The fourth is more difficult. Unfinished, and therefore open to revision. Each day could become the image. For now, I choose to see a woman opening a letter, her hands tearing at the envelope, her eyes unable to read fast enough. She wants to know it all instantaneously. I see her open letter after letter, finding each time a mind that exists only for her. The letters lead, inevitably, to the moment when she sits on the deck of a house in Maine. They lead to Virginia Woolf and nights of Scrabble and never mind that in between there must have been pain and an intricate weaving of lives that must once have been simple.

The fifth is future. A future embedded in the past. It is why we go on. There is always $n+1$ in the equation of desire. Fishing. Yes, I see a man with a rod, and time on his hands, casting the line. The sea both known and unknown, a moving bed of possibility.

This sea hardly moves. It could be blue flannel laid out on an ironing board, or corduroy. Boats skate its surface, leaving lighter lines, like scratch marks on ice. White sails stitch the sea to the sky. No, that's too poetic. The sky and sea meet and color has no meaning. They never meet, except to the deceived eye. And under the sea is a life we can only suspect. Lobstermen rely on that. The steady crawl. The traps, anchored to color. Flutter of gulls. What do they want? Each boat with its halo of wings. Groupies. Scurry and squawk. The noise of necessity.

Bad things come in threes. That's often the case. But that's because we look hard for the third when other things happen by coincidence. In the last few months, two of my friends have lost sons in their early twenties. I try on their lives. I cannot imagine them, though I try. What it must be like, at any time of the day, to feel the future snatched from you. The black shape that forms in the stomach and grows, branching out into artery and vein. The shape in the mind, the door that won't open to reveal that shape, the door that keeps on not opening.

My heart opens to them. And my fear. Where are my sons? William is in France, or is it England by now? Matthew is working on Cape Cod, pulling lobsters out of boiling water and waiting for college to begin again. They walk through the door in my mind and it cannot stretch around their absence. Don't let me be third. Hedging of bets. Bargaining with fate. I leave the number where I can be reached, penance in advance—so it won't be needed. I can be reached here, in Maine. *Don't call. Don't die.* I am my own fear of the future.

. . . always expressing itself. The mind will not shut off. Close the eyes—still, the mind sees, hears, reacts, and moves effortlessly through its worries, back and forth, making plans. It knows what *could* happen. In and out, in and out, the mind expresses its sense of the self. On and on until I'm tired of it, my own internal voice with its interminable comments, its asides, its sarcasms and justifications.

A cloud, and the sun is snatched from the sky. Suddenly I am cold. I open my eyes. Several clouds, a slow-motion swirl, mixing then parting like lovers. Lingering. The sea is mottled with shadow and sun, a patchwork sea. The clouds are seamless—one large cloud where before there were many. No definition, and yet they had such distinct shapes, seen in an instant, frozen in the lens.

I am cold. My nipples stiffen. Do I imagine that the lobster boat circles one time too often, hoping for a glimpse as I stand to go indoors? "Jesus. Summer people. No shame." I doubt he cares what happens on shore, which women are sunning themselves on the decks. He's intent on the ocean. All present tense. Straight lines, therefore and thus. Male to the hilt. He's a fine-tuned machine, listening, working the boat close, a deft motion as he cuts the engine and reaches for the buoy. The trap reveals itself—his stock goes up or down in the blink of his eye.

My life loops and I sit, at its cusp, looking in both directions. Looking back is filled with people and events like a braid of colored ribbons. The future tails off and recedes into mist, the frayed end of possibility. I feel the burden. What do I make of the past, that the future may unfold with some definition? I am like anyone else. I want the end to complete the circle. I want to lay the incessant voice to rest. I want to know that life was not quite random—that I found a way to make some meaning. Like a good short story.

But if there is one thing the past has taught me, it is that our stories do not end. They intertwine. They are messy and incomplete.

I am fifteen and I do not know how to stop my grandmother from voting for Richard Nixon. It seems imperative that I do this, but I don't know how. I do not know that this will be one of my few memories of my grandmother—my agitation at her failure to like John F. Kennedy. That, and the inside of her refrigerator: gouda cheese, lettuce, half a tomato—not the refrigerator of a grandmother, the refrigerator of a Republican. And the box full of flowers. A surprise, such bounty of color from such a spare life. And those stitches. The pinched, parsimonious workings of a lifetime.

I do not know how to end what is ending. Mary Agnes is reckless—with my feelings, with all of us. She drops us quickly, as though she can't be bothered with our silliness. Our pitiful attempts to be daring, the cigarettes, the gossip. She spends all her time with Larry and his friends. Sometimes she drinks. We've smelled it when they come in from driving around. Wears a leather jacket. Acts loud. Acts as though she knows something we don't, and we're convinced she does. Sex. We're sure of it. Something changed and one day her eyes were different, as though they had been satisfied and then stoked—a fire waiting to burst into flame. She is brittle and beautiful and beyond us.

Tonight I am washing dishes when the phone rings. There's so much confusion on the other end. What comes over me now is not the present tense of what *was* but the past tense of what is. The phone rang. It was a friend. "There's been an accident." An accident at the lake, five or six kids, most of them dead. Mary Agnes was not dead—she'd been taken to the hospital. Her parents were on their way.

23

She would not die, of that I was certain. She had that kind of uncanny luck. Others would die, but she would live to make a story of it all. She was that kind of person.

She would not die, but she did. A screaming death, everything mangled and broken, her glasses embedded in the dashboard, her dark eyes riddled with glass. The imagination cannot go far enough with what happens inside a car that leaves the road at high speed and flies, at a thirty-degree angle, without a brake mark on the road, into a tree, shearing the roof and snapping the necks of four people in the back seat. The imagination cannot relive the moment of confusion when the girl who was steering realized that the boy who was working the pedals was not pushing on the brake. When she knew that she was out of control.

I am fifteen and my best friend is dead. The town is in shock. Six of its students are dead, and one of them is my best friend. My phone rings and rings. At school the kids swarm around me. My moods are measured. How am I taking it? How am I doing? It must be so awful. They try to imagine. They are so full of sympathy I am filled with it. I am so important. I have never been so important. I am full of something so powerful that I name it grief, although I had always imagined grief to be something personal and hard, like a fist. This is soft and cloudlike but it spreads its own kind of clarity. I reel with my secret knowledge of what really happened. Of course it is not my secret alone— there are others who rode with them while she steered, while he let the speedometer creep higher and higher, others who shrieked their new freedom and their reckless disregard into the night. But we see no point in telling adults. Her parents would only grieve more. No one would spring back to life. Our secret is ours, a whirling, heady part of our grief. We twist and twist it into a brittle strand of youth. They are ours. The loss is ours. We own it.

I don't know if what I am feeling is grief. There is no room to feel anything but this steady attention. I do know that this attention is close to desire—and that I want it more than I want Mary

Agnes. That it brings with it relief. I will be her best friend forever.

In the past tense she died. I am the woman who lost her best friend, years ago, when she was fifteen. Her story ended. It was different from mine. My story goes on, carrying a small part of hers with me. But in *my* voice. Seen through *my* eyes.

This memory I am forced to reconstruct, brick by brick. Then he said. Then she came. Then they asked. Then we didn't. Today she dies in memory, and again I do not know what to make of it. It cannot be the simple narrative. *Once upon a time I had a friend. She was young and beautiful and a tiny bit reckless and that led to her death. The End.* If she had not died, she would have her own memory to pull out and mull over and then tuck away again and go on. She would see her life stretching before her, a future that curves back occasionally, like this, but holds out its essential promise with no strings attached. She would shiver slightly and stand up. Go inside.

The sea is deceptive with its surface of alternate sun and shade. Look, I say, what do you want from me? My hems are all straight. No stones in my pockets. I'm trying . . . Trying to make sense of it all. Right now, two men are beginning a campaign that will take them each around and around the country. Next year at this time, one of them will be president. Although it seems to me that it matters desperately which one it should be, next year, whoever it is, I will have gone on. The country will have gone on, just as it did when my grandmother put on her stockings and best black shoes and probably voted for Richard Nixon. The sea will rise and fall. The engines will cut the morning in two, and I will see everything with a brief clarity, and then that, too, will cloud over. I will be one year older. Nothing else?

I am fifteen. In two months I will be sixteen, and in four years I will taste the first of those five desires. Three years after that I will have a son, and then another. I will nearly live the life my mother planned for me. I will watch her die slowly and I will wish for her another death, an alternate ending. I will plan my own as though such things could be planned. I will follow the thread that brings me here, above the Atlantic, as though this were ordained. I will feel the future riding the air, the way I imagine it must be to fish the surf. The wrist flicks, the line spins out and rides its own thermal, motionless for an instant before it settles, tugs against the current and is reeled taut.

I am fifteen and this is my first time inside a Catholic Church, inside the deep vault of Our Lady of the Immaculate Conception. I sit nervously with four other girls. Self-conscious. Alive. We do not know what to expect of a requiem mass. We are not prepared for the chanting, the kneeling and crossing, the stifling odor of incense. Father Rogers intones the words he has memorized for such occasions. Father Rogers would not want Mary Agnes to be here, lying in the coffin in the front of the church, teasing us with her silence. I do not want to be here, wondering whether to kneel to something in which I do not believe. Little red swirls before my eyes. I sink beneath the hardwood floor where it is dark. Where night has fallen on the foundation of the church and children are calling—the high, chirping voices of children at play.

I inch myself out onto the plank and I run, all the old patterns intact, memory triumphant, turning and twisting through time, over the black cellar hole toward the maple tree. *Allee Allee in free.* I am safe. My children are safe. It is now.

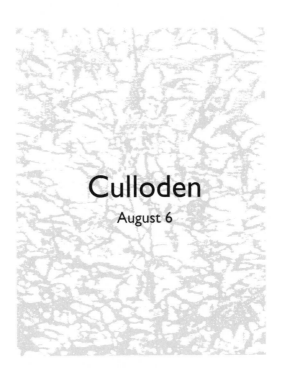

Culloden
August 6

This is where Scotland's dream was dashed. Windswept moor, purple with blooming heather. Bog land. Our shoes keep sinking into watery peat. We wander this high stretch, shading our eyes to see the mountains in the distance. From here, you could sight your enemy. You could prepare.

At first they are imperceptible, a part of the natural terrain. Then the eye discerns a series of long, low, grass-covered mounds. Near each is a plaque: Clan Chattan, Clan Cameron, MacDonells of Glengarry. And behind these, more—then more. The mass graves of men without names. Buried together, identified only by tartan.

It's not hard to imagine: 1746, the field strewn with corpses and Bonnie Prince Charlie already headed for the sea and Skye. You hear the whistle of wind over grasses. A silence like this one. Under foot, the treacherous water. Bog land. Hardly fit for farming. Hardly worth fighting for.

Time is the trickster. Today I woke up half a century old. I am not ready. Too much yet to do. Too much everyday living. Too much left unsaid, unimagined. Stan gave me a silver pin, designed from a letter in the Book of Kells.

Late afternoon. The sky hunkers down, presses, like a lover, against the land. Small sounds. A far sheep, faint barking. Time to drive on, toward Strathpeffer, friends, a phone call from my father.

Late afternoon. In upstate New York, the sun will be high in the sky. The morning newspapers will be screaming my traditional birthday headlines: HIROSHIMA. A kind of national guilt—or, at least, a national doubt.

This land is at the root of my family tree. Duguids and Murrays—"cleared" from these mountainsides—settled in Cherry Valley, New York, in 1774. They left behind their peat fires, their few cows. Left behind the stories—yet to become legend—of their exiled prince.

The road twists upward. In the Scottish summer, the sky never quite goes black, just deeper and deeper blue. We enter its sea. The crofts are all gone now, but there are lights in the few whitewashed cottages we pass. Few. And far between.

They moved on to Ohio and the flat lands of southern Michigan. Their farms flourished. Not a mountain in sight. The names grew steadily American. My grandmother was Mary Ellen Duguid, but she was called Mayme. Her sisters were Maud and Myrta Belle. The boys, John and Dennis and Otto. Stories begin to attach themselves to the names. Soon they come to me firsthand. Mayme marries blue-eyed Benjamin Pendell—the grandfather I will never know. One summer day he will fall from the hay wagon, dead before he hits the ground. Mayme's granddaughter will live for two years in Scotland. She will marry a man she meets there. They will have sons. Thirty years later, she will return with someone else. There will be lights in the cottages, human constellations.

Early evening. At home it is full afternoon. Hard to keep track. Three hours earlier, in Seattle, where William and Matthew now

28

live, newspapers again shout the words on every corner. My sons glance at the headline and walk on. It means almost nothing in their lives. It was my birthday. I was four. It was two centuries after Culloden.

And farther west, across another ocean, the sun is rising. Already August 7th. The dead remain silent. We cannot imagine what it is to cease to exist. The body knows only its own watery weight, its heaviness. It burrows into the amorphous mound on the hilltop where it is at home. Memory makes it all one silken thread. Tie the knot anywhere: tie it in 1774. Then thread the needle and pull it across water. Let America begin. Let the crofters find themselves a farm they call their own. Let them marry and die. At Culloden, soldiers sank in marsh, struggled up again, thrashing, slashing, a chaos of color and sound and foolhardy pride. Over Hiroshima, the plane burst through a seam in the sky—a glint, and then a blinding flash. The earth has learned to live with us. It accommodates bone, shadows burned in stone.

Robert Jimmy Allen

When I was five, my name was Robert Jimmy Allen. It was a name I chose carefully, taking it from my three favorite boys. Every morning I rode in to kindergarten from my home in the country with Mrs. Davenport, the third-grade teacher. At 11:30, I spent a half hour sitting in the small desk next to hers until the class was dismissed and she could drive me home. For thirty minutes, I listened, watched, and secretly learned to read and do arithmetic. I kept my eyes open. I saw Robert, Jimmy, and Allen.

I was five and I lived in the country without many playmates. My father was a physicist, a socialist, an atheist—not in any given order. He believed I could do anything. It did not occur to him that my sex was a limitation. It did not occur to me. He built me a pulley so that I could haul utensils up to my sandbox on the top of the chicken coop. He let me climb trees and swing higher than I ought to until the whole metal frame lifted in the ground, shuddered.

When I came home from kindergarten, I announced that, from then on, I would only answer to my new name. For several months, I became someone else.

———

I now realize I was learning to read in several ways. Learning to read the society, the systems already in place, the language of power. But I was also learning to read myself—and what I found there was the desire for new (vicarious) experience. I chose Robert Jimmy Allen. He was my first experience of entering a story, of literature.

Looking back, I do not see him as symptomatic of something amiss. I do not regret that I did not choose a female name. I do not think it was from lack of role models that my eyes lit on those three boys. Their collective life seemed possible to me. I tried it on. It fit.

———

I am nine. I own the highest spot in the tree. It is mine by right of courage. No one else can climb that high. I look down on the backyard world of childhood. My mother only ventures into it to call us in from baseball games, cowboys and Indians, neighborhood intrigue. She does not know about the secret-compartment rings, the furtive forays across the forbidden railroad tracks, the time we lost Joel Sundquist's father's hammer. She calls us in to dinner.

———

Her voice comes now, clear and distinct. I do not know what it meant to me. The tree was so tall I could lose myself in the branches. I could refuse to answer, watch her move small below me, shading her eyes, peering up.

There is a time in a girl's life when she is most masculine, when she feels power in her body, a sense of flight. It is so fleeting, she almost misses it. Turn around once in your strawberry dress and it's gone. If I were another kind of feminist, I'd like to think that was the time she was most feminine, but part of me knows that's not true. Something happens to the body. I don't

31

want to deny the physical. Being female is not, it seems to me, a construction: it's a fact. It comes with blood and fluctuating hormones and birth and much much more. It's a state of being as well as a state of mind. What I hid from, at the top of the maple tree, was the world I would climb down to—the woman I would inevitably become.

———

By fifteen, I liked the feel of the corduroy skirt swirling up around bare legs. I liked the feeling of being center stage, all eyes on us. "Joe Strzepek, he's our man, if he can't do it—Blencoe can." Each cheerleader in turn, whirl and kick and, at the end, a soaring, back arched, body launched into air. I didn't have to tell myself to like this. I simply did.

I also liked to sit on the hot-air register, reading. This was a secret vice, one I kept to myself. I picked my authors carefully, reading everything the local library had on the shelf. That was the year I read Hemingway, Fitzgerald, Faulkner. They were mine—every glittering flapper, every tough-skinned soldier, every trapped Confederate. I took them so wholly into myself that I could feel them move, like a kicking fetus.

If I identified with any character, it was an identification removed from my experience of the world. These books *were* my experience of the world. They took me out of myself. Caddy— her very absence set the heart in motion. I *was* Caddy, haunted by her moment in the tree, by what she had seen. With her, I slid down the drainpipe and out and away, opening the rich field of imagination.

I hoarded the heat. Everyone complained. (Come set the table. Why don't you clean your room?) I did not talk about what I had come to understand. I brushed out my pin curls, found my red lipstick, slipped into my blue and white jacket, ready for the game.

———

I search my early years for clues to how I became myself. What I see is fairly ordinary. As in all stories, there are places where my experience is unique.

My father, for one thing. I do know that his message was always one of equality. He was more interested in what I was thinking than how I was looking. I don't remember him telling me I looked pretty. (I want to be called beautiful.) I do remember his pride when I'd argue with him.

My mother, for another. It seems to me now that she was a bright, frustrated woman. There was more in her than her circumstances would allow. She had worked her way through both high school and college. Education was her passion. (Next to cleanliness.) She was a good, kind woman. My sophomore year, she took in a girl in the senior class. Pat was the eighth of twelve children, told by her mother to quit school and find a job. For that year, my mother nurtured someone who must have seemed to her more like herself than her own daughter was. She helped Pat go to college and, for twenty-five years, Pat has been a first-grade teacher: my mother's legacy.

My teachers. For the most part widows or spinsters—and tough. They always acted as though I would, as a matter of course, perform for them. Write the stories. Decline the nouns. Do them proud. They never once gave me the impression that, because I was a girl, I was lost.

———

Professor Munford's back was straighter than any of his precious Puritans. A spare man, tall, uncomfortable. He had two pairs of glasses and he absent-mindedly changed them as he switched from talking to us to reading from the poems. Every once in a while he was in transition and his blue eyes went glassy, squinting as though there were something out there yet to come clear.

There was. We were, as a class, coming to terms with what it meant to read a poem. He was open, generous, took our work seriously. He divided the class into four groups and assigned us each a poem. We could write one page only. His most frequent comment was, "Is this the word you mean?" Often he read to us from the work of some former student. I wanted to be in that pile—the pile of papers he might someday want to quote. He was opening up a whole new world. Once again, it did not occur to me it was not mine for the taking.

———

In my senior year of college I married, changed my major from mathematics to American literature, learned to budget and cook, directed two plays, discovered just how much I loved poetry. In 1963, we were reading not only Williams, Frost, and Stevens, but Delmore Schwartz, Theodore Roethke, John Berryman, Robert Lowell, Elizabeth Bishop. "Too bad," my beloved professor told me, "you have such good ideas but no vehicle for expressing them." Possibly this was my first encounter with the male academic standard. Possibly I was just what he claimed—a bad writer, one who could not communicate what she intuitively knew about the poem. I only know that desire is more than dream. With a physical intensity, I wanted to be able to speak about the poems I loved. I wanted to make them come clear for someone else.

Today, I believe, Howard Munford would have spoken to me about graduate school. Would have encouraged me. But I was married (too bad) and my fate was summarily sealed. I spent the next eight years working while my husband studied. I had babies. After that, we went to Brazil. I lost the young woman who loved poetry. She receded so successfully I forgot she was there. She was buried in womanly concerns—real concerns—food and laundry and the occasional pleasure.

Today, I believe, we would deplore the circumstances that led that young woman to put aside her own desires. But I was wholly complicitous. It never occurred to me. It never occurred to my husband. It didn't occur to my erudite professor, my socialist father, my passionate mother. Quite honestly, it didn't occur to the society at large. I had two babies in diapers when Gloria Steinem hit the newsstands. We were the same age, but on opposite sides of the cusp. I had married early, rushed into a world that was waiting to buoy me along. The other world was on hold—and I had no idea how to get back to it.

———

All semester I rode my bicycle to campus to take a class while my younger son was in kindergarten. This time I brought to it not only love, but a kind of hard-earned knowledge. I knew what it meant to reach for the ineffable. My final paper looked at the use of poetry in the plays of T. S. Eliot, Archibald MacLeish, and Harold Pinter. I concentrated on moments when the pressure of emotion forced the language to reach for poetry, when nothing else would do. I concluded that the poet-turned-playwright does not demonstrate this kind of internal necessity as much as the playwright tugged, only half willingly, into verse. Professor Kinnamon took me aside after the last class. "Have you considered getting a Ph.D.?" he asked.

My heart expanded, then settled back, calm for the first time in years. Yes. Until that very moment. And then, with his belief in me, I did not need to get a degree. Could not imagine getting a degree. Could not imagine putting myself at their feet and learning their vocabulary and playing their games.

———

All those years I was jealous. I wanted to be a part of that academic world, the one where I had felt most myself (most recognizably *a* self). I watched my husband go off each day and it seemed to me that my turn would never come. It looked so easy. He'd walk out the door (two tiny heads in the window), turn and wave, then off he'd go, his head swimming in higher mathematics before he even reached the corner. At night he'd return to us, enter our world. He never once seemed to feel guilty, never turned again to see those two faces needing his.

I like to think that, given the right circumstances, given a different atmosphere and attitude, I could have done the same. But part of me knows that the body would have interceded. The breasts spurted milk when the baby cried. It was out of my control. I was held by invisible threads, and it was not just casual housekeeping that let me lick the bottom of their spoons. They were a part of me; I don't believe I could have turned and walked away so easily—and I believe that is part of what it is to be female.

———

When I read Eliot (I grow old), I believe in a unique sensibility. No one else could say it quite that way. No one else would want to. And my job, it seems to me, is to come as close as I can to being that sensibility—for the duration of the poem. To enter its world. To grow old. The nature of literature is individual. The literary "I" speaks from a self; it opposes community. It is the private, briefly made public through the shared medium of language. This is its very reason for being. And this is the tradition I enter (willingly): I decide to add my singular voice to the cauldron of voices.

This singularity of experience matters to me. It is what I write from—and for. To that end, there is no male or female art. To that end, if we submit to all-female journals, we make a statement—we say that we have an agenda, that gender comes before art. However much I might like to be a part of that community, I am not. I climb the tree alone. (My mother grows small. The leaf looms large.)

———

The poets who spoke to me were mostly male. In my case, this was not through lack of female models—though, of course, there were fewer women to read. Dickinson, Moore, Bishop (those precise ladies) spoke *to* me, but not *for* me. In fact, there did not seem to be a poetry of my experience—with the blazing exception of Plath. And Plath was misread, misrepresentative. She had been usurped by the "cause"—thus severed from those of us who knew her work from the inside, recognized each image as interior. It's taken a long while to win her back, to make her wholly individual.

So I settled for Lowell, for Frost and Stevens and Eliot. (Settled? They gave me life!) So I named my loves, and they were Robert Wallace Thomas. I tried them on. They fit.

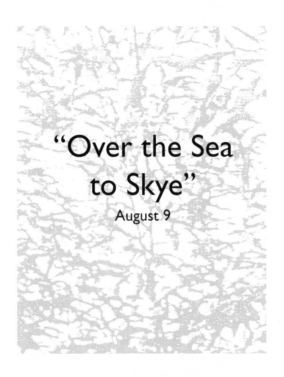

"Over the Sea to Skye"

August 9

Skye is all sky. Huge clouds. Light mist over the Cuillins. A deep, unending blue that begins where ocean ends. Wherever you turn, the sky meets your gaze. It has been here forever, caught between hills. It carries the sound of centuries—bleating of sheep, birdcall, wind. The wind worries at the corners of things, tunnels and dives. It lifts the shutters, rattles doors. Wind sweeps over the cliffs with such relentless force that trees grow only in ravines, away from its onslaught. Wind paves our way as we walk among ruins. All day, wind has whirled in and out of doorways, curled up in hollows, hurled itself headfirst over grassland. *Halloo. Halloo.*

On the map, Skye looks comfortably close to Glasgow, but it's a distance that must be taken on its own terms. So we take the longest route, through Inverness and Strathpeffer over single-track roads, with only occasional "passing places." From Kyle of Lochalsh, it's a short ride on the MacBrayne ferry to the island.

The guide book tells us that the cattle and sheep have no road sense: "As many of the cattle are black, particular care should be taken when driving at night on unlit roads." Black-faced sheep roam freely over the moors, and since it is clear that all the roads are "unlit," we are grateful to see the lights of the village strung out below us as we round a bend. But it's five more miles around Loch Dunvegan to Skinidin where we've booked a bed-and-breakfast.

For a few days, we step outside of time. A walk to the stony headland. Tea, made with water the color of peat. We rise with the sun: eat and sleep as the body demands.

Winged island. Folded in flight. From here, Bonnie Prince Charlie sailed for France. After 1746, the clan system broke down and what the landlords called "improvement" (commonly known as the Clearances) began on a large scale. On the tiny island of Rhum alone, 400 people were evicted to make room for one farmer and 8,000 sheep. They were sent to America, Australia, Canada. Or left on the coastline, like pickings from shipwrecks. The MacLeods, who held the northern part of the island, still inhabit Dunvegan Castle. Their motto is simple: *Hold Fast.*

From the base of the castle, a small boat takes us into the bay. The boatman's face is stoic—he looks as though he's been here for centuries—but in spite of his taciturn style his eyes light up as we steer toward a rock holding hundreds of sunning seals. On the way back, he lights his pipe and stands in the stern, calmly smoking as we head into the wind, soaked with spray.

Each village is a study in simplicity. A trickle of houses, stores, town hall, tiny parish church, strung out along the narrow road that, briefly, changes from one lane to two as it passes through town. A cemetery on the hill. In the post office, the woman at the counter takes her time, talking to everyone. She is genuinely interested in where we've come from, where we're going next. The owner of a small shop not only tells us how he makes his wooden boxes, but offers his opinion on American politics. One phone call from our landlady and we are assured salmon at a local restaurant. Within the town, they know everything that's going on. For other parts of the island, they know what they need. Book ahead for the ferry from Armadale: Saturday's a busy day. With us, they are friendly and courteous. With each other, I notice, they lapse into easy familiarity. Gossip.

We ought to stay. We ought to learn how to live in the here-and-now. But, if I am honest, I have to admit that I would grow bored. Summer would end and the world would shrink to mist and more mist. The days would grow short, and the endless nights would find me sick of myself, caught in a clock of my own making.

The wind is not bored. Lonely, wailing at windows, the skirl of pipes. Looking out, we see the source of the sound. A young man pacing the shoreline, his red sweater billowing. He begins a tune, halts, begins again. His fingers flick the wood. Centuries of song held in the belly, suddenly freed on the wind as though it were its natural medium. High and wild, plaintive.

Stan and I walk down to watch him. He's young—and inexperienced. This is clearly practice and he's a bit embarrassed. Are we from the States? He plays us *Yankee Doodle* then says his fingers are cold. He walks with us back up the hill and disappears into the house behind ours. What does he do when he's not the piper on the shore? He could be anything—mailman, barber, owner of the stationery store. Maybe he's a MacCrimmon (the traditional pipers for the McLeods)—we're only a mile or two from Boreraig where a piping museum now stands on the spot of the traditional piping school. If so, he'll need a modern version of the magical silver chanter from the fairies to make his pipe sing.

Boredom did not enter the English language as a word until half way through the nineteenth century. *Bore*, as a verb meaning *to tire with dullness*, came a bit earlier—in the 1780s, origin unknown. Before that, people were not bored. Or did not know they were.

The people on Skye are united in ancestry, history, hardship, purpose. It was this sense of community that, in 1881, began the Battle of the Braes, the last battle fought on British soil. The crofters of Skye simply refused to pay rent to the landowners. In 1883, fifty police were sent to enforce the law, but they were turned back by islanders wielding sticks and stones. By 1886, there was so much sympathy for their cause that the House of Commons passed the Crofters' Act giving them security of tenure and beginning a system to fix fair rents.

Language carries history. Here the shops are not given names like *Hairtique* or *The Foot Locker.* The Scots prefer a practical approach: *MacLennan's Fruitery, Cuillin Hills Hotel, Skye Ferry Filling Station, An Strupag Cafe, The Pink Guest House.* Names tell what things are—and where they are. While Americans have habitually appropriated such phrases as *Bide a Wee* and *Ye Olde Curiosity Shoppe,* the only example of reverse borrowing is the sign on a jewelry store in Portree called *Tippecanoe.* The bulk of place names on Skye are Gaelic and they are mainly descriptive of a physical feature. *Struan* means "stream." *Beinn Dearg* becomes "the Red Hills." *Camus Ban* is simply "fair bay." *Skeabost, Colbost, Carbost, Orbost* sound singularly ordinary in Norse ("bost" translates into "township") but reveal the island's still more ancient past—a past so full that it's difficult to imagine the people of Skye would ever need to invent a word for boredom.

But if they don't have a word, they have a cure. At the Tallisker distillery we're handed first a large drink of single malt whiskey, then taken down a set of slippery, mist-coated steps to where the barrels are stored for ten years before they are ready for sale. For each year of aging, two percent of the alcohol escapes into the air—what the Scots call the "angel's share."

It is raining. The Cuillins are suddenly nonexistent. The world shrinks to a few yards at each side of the road, the steady clack of the windshield wiper. Farther south, the dark hills and windswept moors give over to lush vegetation. This land was traditionally held by the McDonalds. Huge territorial battles were fought with the MacLeods. Perhaps it was this warring spirit that led so many of the men on Skye to serve in other wars. Ten thousand islanders fought in the Napoleonic Wars and two thousand (one-fifth of the population at the time) fought in World War I.

The origin of boredom, it occurs to me, is simultaneous with the beginning of the breakdown of community. In Skye, never really touched by the Industrial Revolution, communities still exist. People depend on each other in ways that mean they have to get along. The residents have intimacy, and with intimacy comes gossip. With gossip comes interest. They are interested in each other and the details of each other's lives. From the outside, this is so attractive we feel it as loss. We ought to stay long enough to become intimate. To stand in the doorway and pass a few well-worn words.

It *is* loss. I think of contemporary America with its millions of people staring blank-faced at their TV sets while rather ordinary people reveal their most private lives. Oprah Winfrey, Sally Jessy Raphael, Geraldo Rivera, Phil Donahue orchestrate how and when and why we will receive these most intimate of details— details which, in the past, were told over coffee or in back-fence conversation. Details which used to be about people who were *known*. Details which were woven from, and into, the texture of community. Our gossip has gone public. Tabloids scream their headlines. We know more about movie stars than we know of our own neighbors. We've lost the intimate tone of the lowered voice, the underside of gossip that is built on shared values and, along with amazement or disapproval, some empathy.

We ought to stay, but we have to leave on Saturday. Otherwise it will be Monday before we can reach Mallaig. The ferries still don't run on Sunday:

> *The earth is mine, sayeth the Lord,*
> *And all thereto pertains,*
> *Except of course the outer isles—*
> *And they are all MacBrayne's.*

Halloo. Halloo. This word, first used to call ferries from the opposite shore, is possibly the origin of the word *hello*, which only came into common use with the invention of the telephone. The telephone, as we use it today, defines a new kind of community—one of our own making, based on personal preference, a

cat's cradle of connected lines on the larger map. As family members move farther apart, we hold on to them with touch-button
accuracy. Now friends can be selected from a large national pool.
This, however, does not imply the interdependency that fixes
lives in place.

The trip back is much longer, reversing the fugitive prince's
flight from the mainland dressed as Flora McDonald's maid. *Good-bye. Good-bye.* God be with ye. Behind us, the hills withdraw,
huddled under an apron of sky.

Research

There comes a moment when the recollection thus brought down is capable of blending so well with the present perception that we cannot say where perception ends or where memory begins.

—Henri Bergson

[*NEW YORK TIMES MAGAZINE*, SEPT. 1989]

Nonscientists often write of researchers as if all they need to do is switch on their equipment and—presto!—*facts* appear, as if the real work of science consists of fitting such facts into theories.

———

Facts. I have few facts—a child's memory, adult perception, and a handful of letters out of context. Yesterday, the local farmer cut the grass for hay, his distant tractor sawing through the air, and the grass spun out behind him in the meadow in a slow spiral. Today he is there with the baler—this time the rows are straight and he leaves in his wake the sturdy rectangles of bound hay I remember from my childhood. Looking out my window, I smell the interior of a barn, the chaff rising in a late slant of

43

sunlight, the sweet sense of privacy as I climb the vertical wooden ladder to the mow.

I will burn wood in the stove and watch the leaves as they take on the reds, yellows, bronzes, and rusts of New England October. I will take a daily walk to the mailbox, hoping for word from the outside world. Otherwise, I will sit in a light-filled room and allow my mind to drift like the smoke, following the direction of the wind. I will try to fit the facts to the theories, or to make a theory of my own from my own small cache of fact. If I am good at this, I may drift in that current of the past that contains us all, even before the beginning. I may follow it out toward the future where endings may make sense.

———

Memory, so often linked to place, floats free in me. I believe my childhood would have been essentially the same no matter where I lived. What I know of wildflower and winter chill and smell of apple wood burning is merely the backdrop for thought. Thought itself was what we were taught, the thread that bound us all together.

———

JUNE, 1961

I am nineteen, heading for summer school in New York City. My mother wants me to promise I will not go out alone at night, that I will always have someone with me. I do not know what the summer will bring, what opportunities might present themselves. I do not want to promise. I want to be free from the guilt I can already feel. I appeal to my father.

My father rises to the occasion—as I knew he would. There is a flurry of consultation with almanacs and encyclopedias. We look up the population of all five buroughs; we look up the murder rates; we take one-sixth (I'll be there two months). We calculate my percentage chances of being killed. They look ridiculously small. I do not have to promise. Statistically, I am safe.

44

———

My father's name is Bob. My brother calls him Bob because I called him Bob; we have always called him Bob, though we don't know why. Even though I use his first name, that does not stop him from acting like a father. Usually that means constructing a pulley so we can haul pails of sand up to the roof of the chicken coop or taking me for an X-ray when I break my collarbone trying to skin-the-cat on my closet bar. But sometimes it means discipline. That, for my father, means a spanking. Not often, but enough. I am usually surprised when it happens but it's not as if I haven't been warned.

———

I can begin anywhere. My father's father—George Basil Randels—who died when I was fifteen months old, four months before my brother George was born. I don't remember him, couldn't possibly remember him, and yet I have a memory of being lifted, the sharp taste of something new, the tang and sweetness of a lemon lollipop. *Don't tell,* he says. A secret between us.

———

What we didn't figure is how many of those murders were young women. What we didn't figure is how many of them were alone.

———

Bob is a saver. He is sure there will be a use someday for everything. The cellar is full of his carefully sorted savings—stacks of planks, sized and ready, shelving, lead pipes, old bicycle tires, tin cans, and, later, plastic containers. He makes stilts for us out of quart juice cans and rope. We clump up and down the street, ten inches above the ground, pulling ourselves and our heavy feet through the air.

Over his workbench are so many mayonnaise jars that I can't believe we ate that many sandwiches. He nails the metal top into the beam. He fills each jar with nails, screws, nuts, washers, carefully sorted not only for size but for degree of rust. He screws the jar into the lid. Everything is there, above our heads, for when we will need it.

This is not simply habit; it's a philosophy. Here's a letter to his brother William, my Uncle Willy, written in 1952. I have to extrapolate to get the date: his final comment is "Judy is going into seventh grade and is silly as all."

> The problems I am working on are largely of a gadgeteering sort, mechanical design, electrode construction, evaporated films and today the manufacture of "blow out" patches for capacitors. In some sizes we have so much labor in each capacitor that we can afford to reclaim the voltage test failures if the process is simple enough. Well, I etched the "short circuit" away with HCl, baked the thing out and filled the hole with solder glass and it works. Seems like kind of silly work for a "high powered" physicist but that's the way we still do things.

———

I can begin anywhere. With anything. Turn it in any direction. It's all dipping into the same pot. But a pot of my shaping, my hands on the clay. My sense of the past turning toward the present, taking from it what it needs to keep shaping the past.

———

What does my father mean when he uses the word "silly"?

———

[FROM A MS. MEMOIR BY ROBERT B. RANDELS]

Since there was no farm blood in my mother, she didn't really appreciate my father's insistence on buying a farm. It had to be within walking distance from our house in Alma, should have an orchard, and should have a view. Views around Alma are not easy to come by. Any change of elevation of over 10 feet we called a hill and there weren't many hills. But he found 40 acres on the top of a moraine knoll about 2¾ miles from home. The fields were all rented; only a stone basement remained of the former farmhouse but the orchard was mature and contained a wide variety of apple trees and two pear trees. At sunset the view to the West over his own fields from his outpost on a rock near the abandoned cellar gave my father both the thrill of aesthetic pleasure and pride of ownership. The farm boy had returned to the land.

———

So many letters to choose from. How can I know which is important? I can't even decide where I want to sit to write—the glass room closed in by woods, or the large front room with a view that stretches toward the valley, and on, into far distance, hills behind hills in an overlay of time and space.

———

[FROM A MS. MEMOIR BY ROBERT B. RANDELS]

In September, 1925, we took up residence in a third floor flat at Lortzing Str. 2, Freiburg i/Bv, Baden, Germany. After fourteen years of teaching at Alma my father was given a "sabbatical" leave. The farm had been rented to a fairly successful tenant farmer who would deposit any earnings in an account in the local bank, from which letters of credit would periodically issue and on which we would sustain ourselves in Europe. Freiburg had been carefully chosen. It had to be Freiburg because Professor Husserl lectured there on "Phenomenologie" and "Ideen" and was mentor to a whole generation of European intellectuals (especially German physicists) who spent a term under him as part of their Wanderjahr. The physicists had included future Nobel Prize winners de Broglie, Heisenberg, and Schrödinger at least and certainly most of the philosophers of the twenties.

———

What do I know of this time? I know that Willy and Bob had their last fight—in Paris. I know that their younger sister, Margaret, was jealous when the boys went hiking alone in Scotland. I know that ten years later, when asked about the rise of Hitler, my grandfather would assert his faith in the good people of Germany to resist him. I know that, when he died, war was raging.

He did not *think* it could happen. But what did he *feel?* Some things cannot be fit into patterns of thought. Into theories of human behavior.

———

Here is his handwriting. As if from thin air. Someone has recently moved into the house in Alma. Under the floorboards of the attic, she has found a black box. My grandfather was well known in town and the trail leads to my father. Forty years after his father's death, Bob receives this hodgepodge of letters and postcards, some photographs, Willy's baptism records, bank books, notations shifting the past inevitably into the present.

The year is 1906. My grandparents are traveling and studying in Germany. Here is his spidery handwriting, in these records of money spent. Read between the lines. The largest sums are "to Elizabeth, for housekeeping." Sometimes he gives her a dollar for herself, in which case he omits the "housekeeping" notation. He follows his own spending meticulously, carefully writing in each postcard and stamp, even the tip for the coal man ("by request"). He notes the seven cents he seems to have lost. Read between the lines of this man who spends so little on himself that he records streetcar fare and shoe heels. There is the occasional "candy" or "chocolate" or "kuchen."

———

Literally read between the lines. Written vertically up the page, between the column of figures are notes.

48

Herbart-Zellar-Rein pedagogy in America. Must consider it as a product of a German mind, and then as such consider its adaptability for the American Mind.

Way prepared by interest in things German in general. So used to getting good things from Germany that Herbart, once introduced, it was hailed with enthusiasm. The finishedness of its form and answer to burning questions made it especially acceptable to anyone who wished something authoritative to fall back on.

Who is this man with the handwriting that moves, over time, into the German language? *Für Elizabeth, meine Frau* says the housekeeping money. She is more a wife in German than in the intimate language of his thoughts.

———

This memory not quite memory, but vivid, as though the day became a part of the genetic coding. This memory, not a narrative unfolding of time, but a moment in time, the beginning of what we might call recollection. I am walking on the sidewalk, holding a hand. Around me, leaves are swirling—dry leaves, browned at the edges—or skittering across the sidewalk like crabs. Oak and dingy maple, the last holdouts. The day is brisk and I am wearing a sweater. The world opens before me. And then I am lifted to the counter of a store, lifted, and handed a lemon lollipop. Blue sky, red sweater, and a yellow taste. A scratching, dry-leafed sound of seasons changing.

———

What do I *know* I remember? The little events, the ones that no one would bother telling, so I know they're really mine. The apricot tree with its shower of white blossoms. The three-wheeled baby carriage my father made so my mother could push my brother on the long walk to Riesbeck's grocery store. Kindergarten, and my secret name—Robert Jimmy Allen. The way my hair pulled as my mother combed out my braids. Aunt Margaret's wedding and my first pair of patent leather shoes.

Larger moments, fixed forever by intensity. The night is dark and my father's voice is urgent. He lifts me on his back and my mother carries George and they walk through swirling water, reaching to their waists, and then we are sitting on the Erwin's hardwood floor, drinking orange juice, and the water begins to seep through the grate of the hot air register. The women's voices are whispers as they take us up the stairs. The men are in the barn, trying to save the cows. At dawn they come in, silent and defeated. Stupid cows. Too scared to let the men push their heads under water to free them from their stanchions. Stupid cows. Two-thirds of them dead.

The boat comes up over the front porch and noses itself into the front door, right to the stairway where we are plucked from the steps and taken to dry land. My mother doesn't cry, even when we go back home and all the cups in the cupboard are full of dirty water.

———

Bob tells the story in admiration. It's how his brother, my Uncle Willy, decided—no, calculated—that spanking hurts exactly as much whether you cry or not. The discovery came through accident; he was swinging a concrete block tied to a rope over his head. When it lost momentum it crashed against his thigh and he let out a yowl. But the pain didn't stop. So he tried it again— this time on purpose—swinging and crashing, but this time refusing to make a sound. Yes, it was clear, the pain was the same. From then on, when my grandfather felt the necessity to punish, Willy didn't cry.

I don't care much for the science, but I do care about admiration. The next time Bob spanks me, I refuse to cry. At first it's easy—bite the lip and pretend to be somewhere, someone else. But soon, upended on his knee, I feel the usual two or three swats give way to six or seven, faster and harder, and filled with irritation. Finally he breaks into a shout. *Cry, damn you, cry!* I break into tears and it's over.

Judith, 1947, strawberry dress

27	Chocolate & cigar		44			
28	Würzburg		40			
29	Postal u. A		38			
30	Hamums expenses	1	85			
31	Medicine		15			
2	Colonial		10			
3	Karls redk FCM		50			
	To Fürst Leopold F	9	40			
				8	39	81
	Invitation					
	Frau & Gulyás		10			
	Street car & cabm	1	30			
	Lunch	1	05			
4	Baggage		30			
	Railroad & Breakfast	3	00			
	Baggage?		30			
	... to lavatl	1	22			
	Cologne		25			
	Train to Jena	29	80			
	Erfurt Ohrdstahn		45			
	... meine Frau		90			
5	Fed. von Jena		50			
	Post mark und cards	2	00			
	Elizabeth	1	00			
	Libr...	1	00			
6	Elizabeth für Haust	8	00			
	Postkarte		25			
	Vorlesung...		30			
	Christian Robert	8	30			

Left	8	Briefmarken		1	50	
		Hotel & tip	28	80		
		Baggage from SBB	7	17		
		Money				
	9	Baggage	1	06		
	10	...		10		
	10	Stamps		20		
	11	Rudolf von E.	10	75		
	12	Hair cut		50		
		Tipping the coatm				
		by request		10		
		Blumen und Platte		13		
	14	Post Karte		10		
	16	Colonial		10		
	22	First Frankfurt-Dresdner	20	00		
		From Grand betting				
	29	Bon bons		35		
	30	In the museum		10		
	29	Collars		30		
Oct	1	To House betting		54		
	3	"		46		
	"	From Elizabeth				
	"	Post Karte		25		
	5	Street car		20		
	6	From Bank				
	"	To House betting	100	00		
	"	For deposit here	4	00		
	"	Elizabeth	2	00		
		...		07		

William and Robert,
ages 2 and 4

George B. Randels,
Vestaburg, Michigan, 1923

Benjamin Pendell's tractor

Passport photo: George, Elizabeth, William,
Robert, Margaret, 1925

William C. Randels, Princeton, 1931

Robert and Lillian, wedding day, 1937

George and Elizabeth Randels, Mary Ellen (Mayme)
and Benjamin Pendell, wedding day, 1937

isn't far away.
    Quite a number of the
boys have been called to
the army. They slip away
as it were in the night.
At roll call there is no respon
but silence when the name
are called.
                    Your father.

Excerpt, letter from George B. Randels, 1941?

George and Elizabeth Randels, with Judith, 1941

Mayme, visiting on the River Road, 1943

Aerial view of River Road house in flood, 1946

Bob, with pulley on
roof of chicken coop,
1945

William and Matthew, 1968

Bob, 1980

———

To the Editor:

The current fuss over a sperm bank of geniuses reminds me of the story (probably apocryphal) that Isadora Duncan proposed to Bernard Shaw that they combine with the object of producing a child with her body and his brains. But Shaw declined, saying, "The danger is too great—the child might have my body and your brains."

I have doubts of the success of the sperm bank program. Race horses have been bred for speed for centuries, but I compared the record times for race horses and humans and over the last hundred years the speed of humans has increased at the same rate as that of horses. Evidently one gets as good results accidentally as on purpose.

I think the sperm bank for geniuses is going in the wrong direction. Experience shows that progress in plant and animal breeding comes not from selecting the best of one strain but by crossing diverse strains.

W. C. Randels

———

I resolve always to cry.

———

Tenth-grade biology. I love making those squares to predict heredity—the meshing of dominant and recessive until, generations later, you can predict the percentage of blue-eyed offspring of brown-eyed parents. But something in me balks. The chance is for each individual child. Let them have four—even forty— children. They may never see that blue-eyed child embedded in their squares. He will remain forever lost to them, a scientific possibility, hardly real at all.

———

[LETTER TO THE EDITOR OF *THE EXAMINER*]

Mr. Wright:

Trying to teach evolution in the public schools is as silly as trying to teach quantum mechanics or relativity. Evolution doesn't make much sense unless one has an effective understanding of Mendelean genetics and of mutations.

W. C. Randels

Editor's note: That sends most of us back to Tree One.

———

Statistics seem cold and calculated—driving us, each successive generation, into oblivion. The genes swirl and mix, rearrange themselves, the self is effaced in the long sustained order of things.

———

At work, Bob is called "the good Doc." Today he is having a party for the families of the men he works with. He's assembled a motley collection of baseball gloves, a few bats, and balls that have lost all semblance of life. "As good as new," he comments. He's dusted off the croquet set and made wickets out of coat hangers. He's mended the badminton net, tying it in Boy Scout knots that pull and tug at each other in a veritable cat's cradle.

But the racquets are quintessential "engineering." They are all cracked, so Bob has sawed them neatly in two, inserted each half into a piece of copper tubing from the cellar, drilled holes through tubing and handle and "screwed" them together.

Try to play badminton with a wobbly racquet. Aim left, the birdie flies right. It spirals and loops and flops with an English you didn't put on it. The game takes on an air of madness. You don't play to win—you play to see what will happen.

———

[FROM A MS. MEMOIR BY ROBERT B. RANDELS]

At Yale I found myself outclassed by my classmates in Physics but not in all my other interests. I attended lectures, seminars, discussions, retreats, sometimes having to flip a coin to choose between the interesting happenings which appeared almost daily in the Bulletin. I hiked with the Yale Outing Club, sailed with some Power Squadron people, heard talks on Geology and Religion and as a season highlight heard John Maynard Keynes in a three-lecture series at the Law School. I heard Billy Phelps give a Chapel Service and saw several original plays by the Drama School during Prof. Baker's last year as Dean. Shortly after the banks closed and Hitler came to power I heard Chancellor Brüning tell about the grand strategies chosen by the centrists and the Social Democrats. In the fall I was involved in Norman Thomas' campaign and heard him speak in New Haven to a large enthusiastic crowd.

I kept my father informed about all these doings, the broadening educational experiences I was having, and was rewarded with several lengthy letters from him; the letters seemed to encourage my all out effort to do everything. Possibly he saw a necessity in my nature to try everything before settling down to serious academic study. I decided to count this year as one more year of undergraduate study, for certainly I didn't have the singleness of purpose shown by the other budding physicists in Palmer Lab.

————

Miss Copeland writes two names on the blackboard and asks us to vote. DEWEY. TRUMAN. I raise my hand. *But where is Norman Thomas?* Miss Copeland, to give her her due, does not hesitate. She writes another name on the board.

This is upstate New York. Dewey wins by a landslide. In the second grade, Norman Thomas receives one vote. But let us say this was St. Louis, or Little Rock, or Alma, Michigan. Truman would win. It doesn't matter. What matters is that Norman Thomas receives one vote in the second grade in which I am a student.

————

[W. C. RANDELS, "ON THE ENCOURAGEMENT OF RESEARCH,"
LOCKHEED, PALO ALTO, CA, JUNE 1961]

However, in the midst of all this brouhaha everyone tends to lose sight of a central fact that Research is damn difficult and the requisite talent very rare. A reasonable estimate would be that not more than five percent of Ph.D.'s in mathematics would have some chance of making any significant contribution. The ratio is probably higher in physics but still not large. It is not surprising then that Research contracts go out to people who not only are not capable of Research but do not do a competent job of data collection and classification.

———

I don't have to make the pieces of the jigsaw fit. They simply do. It's my life, after all—they're supposed to fit. Slip into it. See how easily it covers all the spaces, a little loose where memory gaps, but basically made-to-order by the tailor of time. If it is part of a larger past, then I do not know it as I live it. What I know is the part that turns toward the future, that places this piece next to that until part of the picture reveals itself.

———

[LETTER FROM GEORGE B. RANDELS TO HIS DAUGHTER,
MARGARET E. RANDELS, AT OBERLIN COLLEGE,
OCTOBER 4, 1936]

As to the thesis topics. In themselves I would think any of them good. From the standpoint of freshness the chances of Bergson and French Literature would be more likely. As I have thought that over it seems to me that might be a good but difficult theme. I don't know enough about French literature of the past thirty years. In fact I know nothing about it. The thread one would follow would be that Bergson's philosophy is anti-intellectualistic, is anti-mechanistic. Does the anti-intellectualism run counter to what we think is a dominant French trait—i.e. getting at truth by rigorous logical processes? Bergson expects to find truth by intuition. His philosophy is mystical. He believes that behavior is instinctive in its nature. We act from instinct not from reason. After the act, "reasons" are found or made up. These are really myths. Man invents myths and symbols to explain or, better, to fortify and preserve these outcroppings of the spirit of life. Then when the spirit in its restless energy has outgrown these forms the conservatives and reactionaries and old fogies still cling to their old ways, old myths, old symbols.

————

What if Betty Dalrymple had never run away with Ray Stevens? Then I would have had to come to terms with the limits of intuition. But it didn't work that way. They cleaned out each of the respective joint bank accounts and ran away to Florida, leaving Marge and Lee high and dry. *Don't say I told you so*, my mother warns as she calls to tell me the news.

————

[GEORGE B. RANDELS TO MARGARET E. RANDELS, OCT. 10, 1936]

A Professor of Philosophy at Johns Hopkins, Professor Boas, has always impressed me as a man of good judgment. He writes that Bergson's influence was very marked from 1890 to the war and that since the war the trends in French philosophy have been away from Bergson. He considers Bergson as having a marked effect on art, religion, and literature in France. He considers the novels of Marcel Proust as representing the fruits of Bergsonianism. On the strength of this statement of Boas it might be a good thing to start reading Proust.

————

[GEORGE B. RANDELS TO MARGARET E. RANDELS, DEC. 13, 1936]

Bergson's teaching about time is a very important feature of his philosophy. It resembles Husserl's philosophy of time. I confess I have never been sure that I knew what either of them meant.

I am quite sure that they both mean something quite simpler than I am looking for. Most difficulties in understanding great minds is in looking for something complex whereas truth is very simple like everything else that is worthwhile.

———

[GEORGE B. RANDELS TO MARGARET E. RANDELS]

Dear Margaret,

I am going to try to make a suggestion in reading Proust and other contemporaries. You will want to find Proust's characters developing and behaving like Bergson says is true of the realities. The only character I know the name of is Swann. (He might just as well be Mr. X for all I know about him.) Does he grow out of the past into the present in any way that reminds one of Bergson's assertion? Do his characters exhibit an art of reporting what is happening in what James called the "stream of consciousness?"

Now, among the various theories of knowledge that Bergson reacted against is rationalism. Then Proust as a follower of Bergson will not, well I don't know just what Proust will or won't do. Anyway get that rationalism business well in mind.

———

All these years, risking my reputation, predicting that Alexander Haig is "Deep Throat." Not that I have been the only one to say so, just that my reasoning, until now, has been secret. It's so simple—his voice is like Hal Holbrook's. If you were Woodward or Bernstein, sworn to secrecy, how could you tell without telling? Typecasting, that's how. How do you typecast a figure that is never seen? Sound, that's how. Simple deductive reasoning.

———

56

[GEORGE B. RANDELS TO MARGARET E. RANDELS, MARCH 4, 1937]

Dear Margaret,

I think it alright to change thesis subject if it is alright with the authorities. It will not come under the category of quitting at all. If it does not fit it will be just good sense to try something more available. I see considerable possibilities in the Bergson one but I think it requires a great deal of meditation. You can't just go to work and gather material. It is a theme requiring considerable maturity, maybe some time later.

———

I can begin anywhere, so I begin here, watching the leaves turn imperceptibly, day by day, until now they are brilliant and the hillside has been transformed. The nights turn cold and I am grateful for the stack of wood outside my door.

———

So many letters. Here's a folder, obviously damaged by one of the floods. I can't read the smeared ink, the blurred words gone fuzzy at the edges. Letters bleeding into each other, as if dates didn't matter. I imagine my mother mopping them with paper towels, then spreading them to dry, the house a sea of words. Memory of a man who lived sensibly far from water.

———

[GEORGE B. RANDELS TO ROBERT B. RANDELS, APRIL 1, 1936]

I am going to take the car in and have that noise investigated. I like some noise so I know that the engine is running but I believe this is louder than necessary for that purpose.

———

October 27, 1936
Dear Robert

Just a line to say it is perfectly agreeable to us that you keep the car till November 7. Maybe we will ask you to bring Grandma from Saginaw if she is still there.

And then further to say that we are pleased at the news item in your letter and to say that we approve heartily of your engagement

    and to say that we congratulate you,

      and to say that we like Lillian very much.

Your father

——

[GEORGE B. RANDELS TO ROBERT B. RANDELS]

I got the business-that-you-put-your-foot-on-to-make-the-gas-flow, Oh yes, accelerator adjusted so that it doesn't go 20 miles an hour when wanting it to slow down for the breaks.

I suppose I could continue for a page and a half writing about nothing. I just won't do it.

Your father

——

[GEORGE B. RANDELS TO MARGARET E. RANDELS, MARCH 16, 1939]

Dear Margaret,

I think it is the proper time to send birthday greetings that they may arrive in due season. I think I shall avail myself of the space remaining to give directions for studying Descartes . . .

——

Research

[FROM A MS. MEMOIR BY ROBERT B. RANDELS]

I had been re-confirmed in the church and became a member soon after my twelfth birthday. Everyone did it and no one knew what he was doing. By the time I was fifteen I was an uneasy church member and by nineteen had decided that an unbeliever should no longer be a member, so I tried to do something about it. I went to see the pastor and he told me he could give me a "letter" to some other church but no exit visa, pure and simple. He wouldn't listen to my persuasive argument which included the absolute hypocrisy of my unbelieving membership. So finally I told my father how unreasonable the minister was and from him I got quite a lesson in church law. There was only one way out—excommunication: I said, "O.K., let's get going with ex-communication. Where are the application forms?" "It is not that easy," he said. "Charges must be brought for a serious crime." "Do I have to commit murder in order to get out of this church?" I asked and he told me that not even a simple murder would be adequate. The crime had to be against the church itself. I got the impression that Joan of Arc could not have been excommunicated had she been Presbyterian and I began to think the devil himself, if he existed, couldn't make a case.

———

Bright day—blue sky, crisp air, white steeple behind the maple leaves. Morris dancers on the village green—six men with bells strapped to their calves, six men with ribbons at their wrists, six men waving handkerchiefs or clacking wooden sticks. A weave of sound and motion, a delicate pattern pulled from the air itself. They rise in unison, and for a second the bells are silent. They are suspended in autumn air. In unison they land, the thud of bells, the multi-faceted jangle, begins a rhythm that will carry them into their next step. In and out, over and across, until they've rung the changes, stand once again facing each other where their dance began.

59

Map the movements on the ground, trace thin lines on the grass to show the intricate pattern they have made; it will unfold in a regular, complex diagram, organic, twisting around itself like a ribbon of DNA.

———

[HENRI BERGSON, *LAUGHTER,* TRANSLATED BY CLOUDESLEY BRETETON AND FRED ROTHWELL, NEW YORK: MACMILLAN, 1928]

So far you do not know what it is, but you begin to search amongst your *ideas*—that is to say, in the present instance, amongst the recollections at your disposal—for that recollection which will best fit in with what you see.

———

[GEORGE B. RANDELS TO MARGARET E. RANDELS, NOV. 12, 1939]

I presume Mrs. VerHey is excited about the headlines these days. I am making no prophecies although I don't think it likely the Germans will attack the Netherlands. Several reports I have seen from Amsterdam said that much of this talk was from the English who were trying to stir up more feeling among the Hollanders against the Germans. I hope there isn't anything more to it.

We lost another football game. Maybe we haven't as good a team as I thought. Your father.

———

[EDITORIAL, *THE DAILY CALIFORNIAN,* MONDAY, FEB. 24, 1941]

The perfect answer to an Oklahoma legislator who peers beneath the academic bushes for "subversion" was made by Dr. W. C. Randels, associate professor of mathematics at the University of Oklahoma.

Representative Claude Thompson, Pushmataha county, has several times demanded that the mathematics professor be dismissed for his activity in the State Federation for Constitutional Rights.

Mr. Thompson apparently believes that once a professor enters the academic portals, he immediately loses his status as a citizen. Thenceforth, according to Mr. Thompson's reasoning, professors can no longer join organizations of their own choosing, nor work for the political institutions in which they believe. Their activities, it seems, must be guided by a conception of "Americanism" which precludes "messing around with government."

In great indignation, Mr. Thompson asks someone to "find out what that professor is doing down there at the university."

What Dr. Randels does as a private citizen will have to rely on the Constitution for its justification.

"What that professor is doing at the university" was answered superlatively by Dr. Randels in four highly technical mathematical pamphlets sent to Representative Thompson, one of which begins: On Volterra-Stieltjes Integral Equations: We propose to prove an existence theorem for integral equations of the type (1) $f(x) = g(x) + \lambda \int_0^z f(y) d_y K(x,y)$.

———

[*NEW YORK TIMES MAGAZINE*, SEPT. 1989]

In the 1930's, a prominent physicist named Irving Langmuir coined the term pathological science, or what he called "the science of things that aren't so."

———

My father is away and my mother has taken us to Sunday School. Somehow we understand that this is a secret and that my father would not approve. I am herded into a small room with other children and two ladies in flowered dresses. There must have been more to it, but I remember the crayons, lined up on the table. One of the flowered dresses asks us to draw a picture of God. The other children all reach for a crayon. There is a red one left, and I take it. I do not know what God looks like. What emerges is a clown suit with red buttons, red polka-dots, a ruffled collar and cuffs, a pointed hat. The face is a cloud, featureless, a space to be filled in later. No eyes, or mouth. Just a puff of cloud. The flowered dresses praise other drawings; they tactfully say nothing about mine.

———

Quite a number of the boys have been called to the army. They slip away as it were in the night. At roll call there is no response but silence when the names are called.

Your father

———

AUGUST 6, 1945

Aunt Margaret is home from Ecuador and it is my birthday and she is dressed in long skirts and an embroidered blouse, she has castanets in each hand and she moves through the room singing, clapping, clicking in a strange exotic dance. She puts a wooden bowl on her head and tosses fruit and nuts and shiny coins to the few children in the room. The room spins and the children chase after the prizes.

I don't know when they heard. I must have been in bed when the news broke into their evening radio programs. Some time that evening my pacifist parents and my Aunt Margaret, just home from working with the Department of Health in Ecuador, must have learned what their country was capable of doing. I am sure of this: they sat for a long time in silence. They forgot that it was my birthday. The larger past had swallowed the smaller one whole. The date was etched in history; they sat in silence in a white clapboard farmhouse in upstate New York and watched the sun sink, watched the black sky begin to settle on their world.

———

[MARGARET E. RANDELS TO WILLIAM C. RANDELS, NOV. 4, 1945]

Today I had to teach a Sunday School lesson, and I'm afraid it will be the end of me here . . . Then I have been to church too. The only way I can console myself is to wear a very daring and extreme hat, to shock the hypocrites.

———

DECEMBER, 1945

I'm four and a half and I have decided that there is no Santa Claus. I've tried to believe, I really have; I've ignored the fact that our chimney looks much too narrow, ignored the fact that the Kilmers next door have no chimney at all, even tried to block out the logistical details of how many packages will fit into a sleigh, how many children there must be in our own town, to say nothing of all the towns on the route to Michigan. But I can't ignore the evidence he himself has left. One half eaten cookie, one drained glass of milk with its sticky ring where the cream rose to the top as it waited for him. How could anyone eat that many cookies? More, how could anyone drink that milk, the kind I sit before, my stomach churning, under orders to finish it before I leave the table?

I confront my mother with the facts—all but the milk which might get me in trouble. *Don't tell George*, she pleads, *he's still so little.* But how can I keep, not a secret, but the truth?

———

This is the present, this past into which I delve to discover myself in fading ink. It is autumn. The year does not matter. The trees do not measure time on calendars. It might as well be the autumn of 1942. I might as well be holding my grandfather's hand. The leaves scuttle ahead of us on the sidewalk. They sound like the syncopated scratch of pen on paper.

———

My son William, named for his great uncle William, visits from Boston. Around the dinner table, we hear it for the first time. He takes us into his story until we rock with laughter. This is his memory. Locked in him, his version of his life.

Will's eyes grow wide in the telling. We've left him and his brother for the weekend with a babysitter. The first night, Mrs. Wilder asks William to say grace. "We don't say grace." A series of questions digging deeper into church and God and then an incredulous "don't you *believe?*" William's blue eyes go bluer, his voice insists: *What did she mean, didn't I believe? Of course I believed. I tried to tell her. Look, I believe that is my dog. I believe that is the driveway. I believe it's eight o'clock. She just couldn't get my point.* His voice is full of relived indignation.

———

["BRAGGING RIGHTS," ROBERT B. RANDELS, COLUMN IN *THE ELMIRA STAR GAZETTE*, SEPT. 11, 1980]

Grandchildren are for bragging about. Since only one fourth of their nature is genetically yours, the bragging is not as self-congratulatory as bragging about children.

My 15-year-old grandson shows signs of artistic genius. I was there when at age six he discovered perspective and drew tunnel after tunnel, cave after cave; depth was important and also its representation on a smooth page.

I had to hint to get the painting. It was standing in a corner of William's beer-can-lined room (I helped him collect the cans; I drank some of the contents). I asked when he had started using oil paint and he said that the paint was acrylic.

I couldn't believe it; the tones were subdued, no harsh and garish glaring primaries—unbelievable. When asked how he tamed the medium he said offhandedly, "you just have to take the time to mix the colors properly."

I absorbed that shot at my slapdash approach to projects but got to thinking how lucky William is to be going to school where an artist and his technique is recognized almost as much as a jump shot specialist.

———

[GEORGE B. RANDELS, TORN PAGE,
ALMA STATE SAVINGS BANK BOOK, 1906]

If a people were kept busy as the Swiss there were no need of art, but we have leisure and must employ it in best possible way.

———

[LETTER FROM WILLIAM C. RANDELS
TO ROBERT B. AND LILLIAN P. RANDELS]

The question of identity has taken a funny turn. The commonly proposed answer seems to be to merge into the identity of some group. Father used the folk saying "every tub must stand on its own bottom." Like all old sayings, the meaning is somewhat obscure but pursuing the analogy, the current ideal seems to be a lot of round bottom tubs leaning against each other for support.

I think there is a completely different reason for so-called identity problems. In absolute terms, none of us amounts to a whole hell of a lot and this takes a bit of getting used to. The problem is not that people don't know who they are, but that they do know.

One thing our father tried to do with students was to try to make them believe that some talent they may have had was important. He may have succeeded occasionally.

———

In all of this, my mother is absent. My mother, whose sense of fun attracted my father to her. My mother, who worked—hard— all her life. And before her, her father who fell from the hay wagon one summer day before I was born, dead of a heart attack before he hit the ground. And my grandmother Pendell who sold the farm and worked—hard—all her life. She was one of the first members of the International Ladies Garment Workers Union, and then, even into her eighties, she took care of "old" people who were often younger than she was. They left no words by which I can come to know them. Or myself.

———

Is that what I am doing? The old cliché of trying to find my self? Or is it more than that? A way of knowing what makes the self. There are people who pay little attention to who they are; they are saints—or scientists. They speak of "we" as though our function on this earth were communal. They do not know the loneliness of the solitary, narcissistic impulse—know thyself.

———

Bob has a theory. If he fills all the plastic containers in the cellar with water, then puts them all in the crawl space under the kitchen, they will freeze in winter, keeping the kitchen cool on hot spring days, and they will warm up gradually over the summer, keeping the kitchen warm as autumn plays tricks with the temperature. He hires his grandson, William, to help him.

Will returns from this job in great spirits. He imagines some-one, someday, crawling into the space, discovering the bleach and cider and detergent and milk of another century. He imag-ines them all bursting at once, flooding the cellar with water, vintage 1978.

———

I have my best thoughts in the bathtub. The body takes over, nearly floating in memory, the feet finally warm, the mind blurred to a still. The body knows. The mind goes on spinning, but tem-pered by association. I contrive long, convoluted sentences, al-most without syntax, a Faulknerian response to life. Or I shut down. One word. A simple clarification. One word, and then another, held together by the fluid body in which I float.

Don't try to save these thoughts, these almost-sentences. No typewriter. Not even a pad or pencil. Slippery fingers. The whole thing damp and incomplete.

———

Here are Bob's tools, rusting in a pile of mud in a corner of the cellar. We shovel them out, shovel the nails and washers and nuts, turning our faces as we hear the clink of metal on the bottom of the wheelbarrow. It's too hard to imagine washing each one, rub-bing it with oil, feeling the grain of the hammer handles. Too many floods. Once, it was adventure. Something to tell to grand-children. Now, it's one too many. We wheel them to the curb.

———

Leaves hurl themselves against the window. I open the door to choose one for my son Matthew, who is living in Tucson. I tuck it into the envelope. Here is a spot of color, a shape, which, three days from now, will bring these hills into the desert. Will tug at him with his own history.

———

Tonight the moon is so large it seems to roll along the tops of the hills. Yellow. The taste of coming winter. All afternoon, in the pasture below us, cows have made random patterns of black and white, buff and reddish-brown. Like a kaleidoscope, they swirl and mix—a shifting landscape. Now, they lie down in darkness and in the morning, when I stand again at the window, they will not notice me as they make their slow morning rounds.

———

Sometimes I dream a granddaughter. One-fourth mine. One-eighth Bob's. One-sixteenth of a man who was born in 1876. We recede as she carries us into the future. Sometimes I dream her, in autumn, the moon a secret between us.

———

Dear Margaret,
I am glad you had an opportunity to make the acquaintance of Mr. Robert Frost and to know his daughter. I think Mr. Frost is my favorite of the living poets. You will have a chance to see Vermont stone fences, the setting of "Mending a Fence." I suspect the inner reality of the poem can be realized in mending a Michigan fence although a barbed wire fence is not nearly so poetic a setting. The barbs are suggestive of the temper which usually goes with a line fence. I think even I might be more considerate with my neighbor if the fences were stone instead of barbed wire. But I imagine that even stone fences are exasperating—the stones probably do not stay readily where put, and they may bruise one's fingers. Maybe it depends more on the dispositions of the neighbors. Your father.

———

These are the last years of my grandfather's life. His words reach out to lift me up. They are sweet-smelling, and yellow. I am drenched in summer sweat, riding the collective sweep of their sounds. I tumble and slide in the golden haze of summer, store it somewhere where it will wait for me. A day so close to this one.

I, too, wonder at the trail of stone walls that weave through these Berkshire woods. Hundreds of years ago, men lifted them up, balanced them there where they stand, mossy and patient, then turned their backs and headed home. Then headed off, to make new homes, leaving only the wall to testify as second-growth shifts gear, moves closer and closer.

———

[GEORGE B. RANDELS TO WILLIAM C. RANDELS, JULY 12, 1942]

Mr. Staylik's tractor has lots of antics. We are using it in the hay field. It has lots of excuses for stopping operations. He knows most of them. He is expert at interpreting all its varying sounds. When it threatens to expire he knows where it needs a tap with the end of the fork handle. Now it will be one spot again another, usually in the neighborhood of the carburetor or feed line. Sometimes it is a light tap other times quite a blow, and sometimes the tines are what is needed.

There are occasions when the pitch fork availeth not. It stopped on the road and emitted a cloud of smoke like a picture of a miniature smoke screen. That turned out to be due to a leak in the gasket and water sprayed on the bearings of a connecting rod which crystalized. It took him a couple days to make the repair.

These days give me a chance to recover from any oncoming fatigue. We are making twenty acres of hay on shares on Bartley's. There are seven of very heavy hay on our own place.

———

November—grey sky, the earth rocks itself to sleep. Flies die upside down on the windowsills. The woods are punctuated by branches of birch and wild cherry. They glisten, then go cold.

This is the season of death, though seed in the feeder brings us a flicker of color. He died, leaving a mesh of memory so fine it makes the tent under which I will, eventually, grow up. I pull it with me into marriage and motherhood. A canvas gone mildewed and hard in the weather. Something I must pass on.

I will wait for a day in early fall when I can stretch it out in full sunlight. I will sweep it with a broom until an odor rises—the lemon scent of August and the throat-tightening taste of September. That's what I'll give away. I'll wait for a girl with yellow braids and a bright red sweater. She will come to me in late afternoon with the sun behind her, her wisps of hair forming a halo, the moment a bar of music, or a hand dipped in cool water, a glint of light as the present lifts the past from its bed.

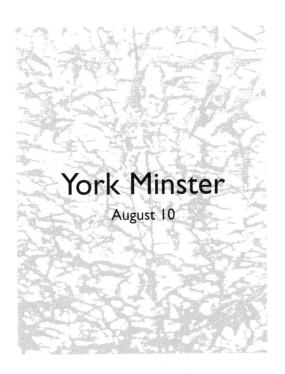

York Minster

August 10

There's scaffolding on the outside. Even so, it's possible to see the elegant lines of the transept, the stained-glass windows in their narrow arches. And inside, the air is green, like the interior of a forest. A children's choir. Soprano. The voices fill the nave and spill around corners. They reach for clarity, hold its long note, descend to the still point of silence.

This is religion. The pure compulsion to praise.

This is religion as I would recognize it. Art, and the forms of art, a formal feast of sound and sight. High atheism, my friends call it. Whatever it is, it stirs. It throws logic to the wind.

That is, until we discover it on the West Wall—the epitaph to end all epitaphs:

> Yf wisdome wealth honor or honesty chastity
> Zeale faith hope or charity
> Yf universal learning language law
> Pure piety religions reverend awe

Firme friends, fayre issue; if a virtuous wife
A quiet conscience a contented life
The cleargies prayers or ye poore mans tears
Could have lent length to mans determind years
Sure as ye fate wch: for our fault wie fear
Proud death had nere advancd this trophe here
In it behold thy doom thy toombe provide
Sr: Williã Gee had all these pleas yet died

We walk out into startled daylight, the streetsong of air compressor and jack hammer. Above us, the chink of chisel on stone. A web of disembodied voices. "Find t'pub, luv?" Flick of cigarette. Footstep on pavement. Our imperfect paradise.

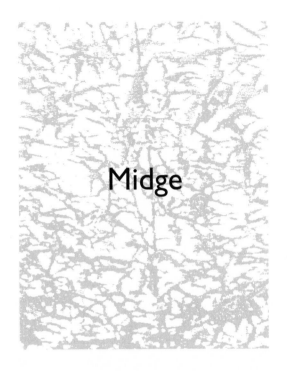

Midge

Alfred Hitchcock's Vertigo *(1957) is widely considered to be a masterpiece. The film is a deconstruction of male romantic fantasy. In it, Scottie (Jimmy Stewart), a former police officer suffering from vertigo, is hired to watch his old school chum's wife, Madeleine (Kim Novak), who is said to be suffering an obsessive identification with Carlotta, an exotic woman who committed suicide in the last century. Scottie becomes increasingly infatuated with Madeleine and, in the wake of her "death," he suffers a breakdown. In fact, Madeleine (and Madeleine's version of Carlotta) are played by "Judy" (also Kim Novak), a red-haired girl from Kansas hired as part of an elaborate murder plot. Released from the hospital, Scottie accidentally meets Judy and, noticing the resemblance, tries to make her over into the lost Madeleine. Her transformation is complete, but the result is tragic. Scottie's loyal friend and former fiancee, Midge (Barbara Bel Geddes), watches from the sidelines, unable to help him as he is pulled deeper and deeper into this complex of deception and desire.*

Roger Park's dark hair is pushed back in what we called a "duck tail" or a "D. A." We don't say duck's ass out loud. He has used just enough grease to hold it in place, combing back the sides to the point where they meet, forming a tail, a cocky grin. Roger Park is fifteen and I am only twelve and a half, but we share the long bolted-down rows of the seventh-grade classroom. Each day I stare into the back of his head, and each day he finds some new way to make me aware of myself.

As if I didn't know I was changing! I've watched each new half-inch of breast as it emerged from those awful days when it was all nipple, nubbed, noticeable under everything but sweatshirts. Now I have tried every way I can think of to make my mother THINK BRA. I've left the Sears & Roebuck catalog open to the page marked "brassieres"—left it not on the coffee table or couch, but on the floor by the register where I do my reading, where she always picks up my magazines even when I'm not finished—but this time it has stayed in place for two straight days. Open and glaringly unread. She is clearly ignoring my hints, carefully avoiding having to say what she finds so hard to say. She was like that over Kotex, but now I've grown steely as I buy my own, even when there's a boy at the checkout counter and I can feel my face flush and my eyes go glassy.

These are the same eyes I use to look at the back of Roger's head. He makes me die a little bit inside. Part of it is hate. His eyes roll over me as I walk to my seat; he notices everything, whispering "niblets" or "limp lips" or, worst of all, "brain." Part of it is pure desire. I dream about the day when I wear my new bra—*if* I ever have one—under a fuzzy pink sweater set. I will accidentally bump into him as I slide into my seat; one breast will brush across his arm, making the black hairs stand up ever so slightly. I will do to him what he has done to me.

How can I think about arithmetic? Geography? Diagramming sentences? I am bound up in boys, not books. I am blood and bubble gum, each day an agony of wanting.

By early spring, end of the basketball season, when Roger Park walks me home one night and presses my back against the tall pine in my back yard, pulling me roughly into his leather jacket, when I feel him hard against me, raw and unfinished and urgent, the wanting finds a form. But his lips scare me. They are hard— even cold—and they are too old. They would pull me into the darkness, take me spiraling down until there was no future— only a present so intense it would strangle. He is too old to be in the seventh grade, too dumb, too disadvantaged. I have outgrown him without even learning what I am desperate to know.

While I am smarting under Roger's black eyes, Sylvia Plath is recovering from her first attempted suicide. She is pulling herself, by sheer will, from under the crawl space of her mind—the thing she fears the most. She is turning, once again, to the world outside. By the time he pins me against the pine tree, his hands moving over my breasts, his ropy penis thick and demanding on my thigh, Sylvia Plath will be back at Smith, all smiles and promise and dazzling dark words. I do not know she exists. And I need her. She is mirror and miraculous sound. I am what she has already lost: *What I want back is what I was / Before the bed, before the knife, / Before the brooch-pin and the salve / Fixed me in this parenthesis / . . .*

Ten years from now, Sylvia will put her head in the oven. Ten years from now I will graduate from college, already married, already primed to work while he gets his degree. I will never once ask myself why I have not gone on to graduate school. I will never even think to think about that. I have what I have been told I want. I have a man, a marriage. Soon I will have children. I will be fulfilled. I know—because of Midge.

Most people, if asked, can't remember Midge—the "other" blonde in Hitchcock's *Vertigo*. She's hardly glamorous with her practical shoes, her no-nonsense manner, her wry outlook on life. Halfway through the film, she walks out—down the length of the hospital corridor, it takes so long—opens the door, and does not return. Swallowed by darkness, she chooses life. Whatever she does next, it does not matter. In the dark theater, we follow Scottie circling and circling, chasing not the ghost, but the ghost of a ghost—a woman ephemeral as air itself. A woman more idea than substance. A vapid blonde Kim Novak kind of woman—the kind Hitchcock himself desired—and the camera's eye looks and lingers, touches her grey suit, her perfection. Never mind that she dies. Never mind that love is defeated. Love is not the issue here—it's obsession, it's all-consuming desire.

Sylvia is a Midge. She is bright and energetic and competent. She makes things happen. And she worries. What man would have her? Over and over, her journals examine her fear: how to be successful *and* keep a husband; how to be bright and capable in a world where men want something else; how to need, without giving up her self. *I think this book ricochets between the feminine burbling I hate and the posed cynicism I would shun. One thing, I try to be honest. And what is revealed is often rather hideously unflattering. I want so obviously, so desperately to be loved, and to be capable of love. I am still so naive; I know pretty much what I like and dislike; but please, don't ask me who I am.*

High school. I have recently given up white bucks and crinolines, just as, before that, I shed dog collars and poodle skirts. Now I own a closet full of tight tweed skirts, blouses with round collars, circle pins. They look so innocent. I dance slowly around my room to *he was born / the next of kin / the next of kin / to the wayward wind* or *Oh my papa / to me he was so wonderful.* The lyrics tell me how I feel. I hold myself close, imagining Elvis with his unruly lock of hair, his sultry lips, as he cradles the microphone, croons the flip side of "Heartbreak Hotel" until I'm convinced that, yes, he was the one who taught me to kiss. Each night I curl my hair, sleep on bobby pins, wake up hoping that nothing has gone wrong. When I comb it out, I know how my day will be.

Liz Taylor is getting Eddie Fisher away from Debbie Reynolds, who appears cherubic, round-faced, wronged, in pin curls and house robe— Mike Todd barely cold. How odd these events affect one so. Why? Analogies? I would like to squander money on hair styling, clothes. Yet know power is in work and thought. The rest is pleasant frill. I love too much, too wholly, too simply for any cleverness. Use imagination. Write and work to please. No criticism or nagging. He is a genius. I his wife.

In the mirror, the frantic face of my generation. Don't ask us who we are. We might tell you. We might tell you what it is to pretend we don't know the answers in class, to pretend to be dumb so the boys will ask us out. We pretend other things, too, in our strapless gowns and rosebud corsages, our gossip and giggling, our perpetual simulated sophistication. We burst through the door asking what Teresa Brewer sang tonight on *Your Hit Parade*. We could *be* Teresa Brewer—but her voice betrays her; there's something dark and hidden. Something more like the furtive back seats of cars, the rough-and-tumble petting on the floor of the den, the sexy dream that leaps from the screen and seduces us all.

Let me be strong, strong with sleep and strong with intelligence and strong with bone and fiber; let me learn, through this desperation, to spread myself out: to know where and to whom to give . . . Not to be bitter. Save me from that, that final wry sour lemon acid in the veins of single clever lonely women.

We need Sylvia, but we get Midge. Sylvia gets Midge as well. Even Midge gets Midge, in the shape of Barbara Bel Geddes. She can't escape her identity. There she is, wearing glasses, clean and articulate and so wholesome as to be *un*desirable. What can she do? She cannot change. That's for Kim Novak, for Hitchcock himself, for every girl in every darkened theater across America. We sit in the back row, the boys' arms casually draped across the back of our seats, watching Midge lose Scottie to . . . to what? We do not yet know that Jimmy Stewart is caught in the maze of deception, caught in the fake Madeleine's portrayal of the elusive Carlotta. He is taken in by the nosegay, the cemetery, the mansion and monastery. The haunting beauty of someone haunted. We look at the way he looks at Madeleine looking at the portrait of Carlotta. We watch as Midge watches his fascination. And then Midge does the all-too-thinkable—she paints her own portrait, putting herself in Carlotta's gown. It's awful. Even the audience can tell how wrong it is. She is a parody. "You fool," she tells herself. You fool.

At the other side of the camera, Hitchcock's jealous eye roams the set, following Kim Novak. Distant and seductive, she is everything we can never be: her voice a dusky whisper, her grey eyes mysterious. She winds herself up on a spool, the re-made Madeleine over the vibrant Judy over the ethereal Carlotta over the falsely vulnerable Madeleine. Our hearts race as we climb the tower with her. Startled, we stumble. We fall. And go on falling. So hard to remember the red-haired reality underneath the blonde apparition. So hard to hear Judy's voice, coming from the netherworld of Scottie's creation . . . Hitchcock's creation, whirling him on the spindle of his own obsessions.

Who is Midge? She is a single, clever, lonely woman. Textbooks tell us she is the "mother figure." No man wants another mother—we're told that too—if not by books, by the men themselves. But what's so "motherish" about Midge? She is bright (oh yes, she went to college, that's where she was engaged to Scottie "for three whole weeks"). She is capable—she designs brassieres, without embarrassment—a practical woman who accepts her own body. She is strong—is that what turns her into a mother?

Men don't want Midge. They don't even want Judy—an honest-to-goodness girl from Salina, Kansas. They don't even quite want Madeleine, for all her vulnerability. Nor do they want Carlotta—it's "Madeleine" who wants to be Carlotta, the tragic heroine of her own obsessive story. Men want the space *between* Madeleine and Carlotta; between reality and illusion lies the dream. The imagination set free. They can slip out of their names and into the maze of desire.

No, they don't want Midge. She asks them to look up or down, to look into the face of weakness, to accept their fear of heights. She asks them to want her without subterfuge. She blows out the candles and turns on the lights. She stands before them—in her glaring equality—and dares them to want what they already know.

What alternative does Midge give to Sylvia? *Get a nice little, safe little, sweet little loving little imitation man who'll give you babies and bread and a secure roof and a green lawn and money money money every month. Compromise. A smart girl can't have everything she wants. Take second best. Take anything nice you think you can manage and sweetly master. Don't let him get mad or die or go to Paris with his sexy secretary. Be sure he's nice nice nice.* Sylvia gets the message.

You think Scottie went somewhere, conquered his vertigo? He went nowhere. He pulled himself into a vortex of his own making, round and round, sucked to the center. And there we are—down at the bottom with him, stuffing ourselves into the nylon stockings of his dream. We fasten the clasp around our own necks.

You think this is only the fifties? That younger women have freed themselves from the noose? Look at them. They are so blonde, so thin, so overtly aware. Listen to their music. Look at their idols: Come, says Madonna. I will teach you what to want. I will take it all back—the smouldering eyes, the jabs and pinches and callous words. The lust. I will turn it inside out, project it on a larger screen. This is what you're dreaming of? Then let me dream it for you, around you, above you, below you. I will steal your dream. *She's* nobody's fool.

There is rage in Madonna; she gets her revenge. There is rage in Sylvia; she dreams her revenge: *Herr God, Herr Lucifer / Beware / Beware. // Out of the ash / I rise with my red hair / And I eat men like air.*

You think I am most alive in memory brought to life? In Roger Park's rough embrace? Maybe so. Every time he spoke to me, I was afraid for myself. Afraid of who I might become. *Attractive, refined blonde, 36, single white female, M.D. with media background. Enjoys cooking, entertaining, theater, jazz, dance, country inns and foreign travel. Seeks professionally accomplished 33–45, conservative gentleman with contemporary style.* Or: *Pretty, slender Ph.D., late 40s, seeks intelligent, creative, caring man with a twinkle in his eye and a sense of humor, willing to take a risk again [Harvard Magazine,*

1991]. Notice the way they begin. "Attractive." "Pretty." "Slender."

I am still afraid. This summer I will turn fifty. I will disappear, become invisible. I will fade into the countless numbers of older citizens, the people who populate the highways in RVs and crowd together in clean, family-style restaurants. I will buy a bicycle to lose some weight. And I will taste the wry sour lemon acid. Don't ask me who I am. I circle myself, eddies of time and memory caught in the lens. Not the tintype moment held at arm's length, but the past in present-tense, moving across the screen. Larger than life? More real.

Make up an ad: *Smart woman, early fifties, overweight but fun, interested in reading, country music, junk television, not-so-junky food, heated conversation, sex.* Be honest, don't start cleaning up your act. Don't add *rides in the countryside, sunsets over the ocean, Hungarian restaurants, candlelight.* Not that it wouldn't be true, but that it would be truth romanticized.

We do not say what we learned in seventh grade: that we want to be loved, bodiless. Like Sylvia, we *have a self to recover, a queen. / Is she dead, is she sleeping? / Where has she been, / With her lion-red body, her wings of glass?* Is she, like Sleeping Beauty, waiting for the prince? Where *has* she been? She was there once, her dozen years rolled up inside her—every tree she ever climbed, every book she ever read, every early-morning snowfall she walked through her yard leaving a spiral of prints. She felt herself spinning counter-clockwise, transparent and free, before the male gaze pulled her into his orbit. She sleeps now, curled and dormant, waiting for Midge to free her.

But there is no rage in Midge. No lion-red body. For a brief instant, she paints herself into the dream. And then she gives up. Her movement is linear; she knows more than we will ever know. We do not see what she offers us as she walks proudly down the hall, toward the light, out. For the rest of the movie, we wait. But she is gone.

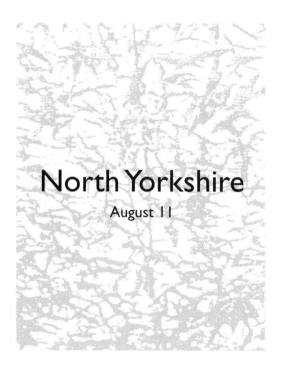

North Yorkshire
August 11

A purple sea. We wade in, but the going is slow. The heather, dense and wiry, tugs at our heels. The sky is so large you are forced to look close—a tuft of sheep's wool caught on a twig, a star-shaped rock, windbitten thistle. In the distance, a standing stone, relict of time. *Suddenly the sky explodes. Shatters into a thousand shards of sound. And then, a second later, the plane appears beside us—at eye-level—skirting the rim of the moor. Another second and it's gone, dragging its shadow across the valley below us.* We look down into lush farmland, a patchwork of walled fields. Serpentine glint of water. Carved by glaciers over a million years ago, today the Dales are widely known for cattle and cheese. Tiny villages carry the river of history in their names: Aislaby, Egton Bridge, Hutton-le-Hole. Here, over Roman remains, the great Norman abbeys of the twelfth century were built. *British Harrier jets, up from Sutton Bank, have recently begun to practice hugging the contours of the land. In the Gulf War, too many pilots were lost.* The ruins have become a part of the landscape. In the fourteenth century, many of the monasteries were stormed by raiding Scots. And to the east, Whitby Abbey suffered naval bombardment in the First World War. For the most part, though, the elements are the enemy. Wind. Rain. Stab of sun. We stop at Rievaulx with its three-tiered walls and massive pointed arches. The third abbot, Ailred, opened its doors to any wanderer regardless of religion. Standing at the base of the columns, one is dwarfed by man's idea of God. From a distance, the open arches frame the sky. It is tamer—and more lonely. *Now, precise as a needle, they maneuver the narrow shafts of the dales.* Five birds rise above the nave; one veers through a window, threading its ancient eye.

Picnic at Paradise

Every night under my pillow the earth ticks
while somewhere in distant country tomorrow
wanders looking for me . . .
　　　　　—William Stafford, "Chicory"

The dark-haired woman in the window seat is reading a book called *52 Ways to Show Your Child You Love Him.* Her son, pale for late July, is immersed in a Bible book, trying to find the hidden Moses in a maze of illustrations. On planes, I drift in and out of my thoughts. I shamelessly eavesdrop on conversations. I'm interested in how other people manage the business of getting from here to there

and there, in this instance, is the state of Washington where both my sons are carving out their lives without me. As is proper. So I make the pilgrimage to *see* where they live. Later, I will be able to visualize the curve in the road, the color of the door, the cold sting of rain, when they tell me over the phone what's been happening. That's what this trip is about—later.

It's not easy to think of the infant Moses without an image of stilled water, bullrushes, the audible oh of discovery. In the boy's book, the baby's hidden, yes, but camouflaged upside down in an intricate branching of trees, waiting to be discovered there, half falling from his little basket. A Bible for modern times—more visuals than language. And when there are words, the familiar, throat-tightening lines have been altered. No "Take therefore no thought for the morrow" nor "Then I saw as through a glass darkly." Outside the window, nothing but cloud, stretching like flat cardboard. Below it, the unseen land slipping away. And on the land, the hundreds whose lives have been altered forever by the flooding Mississippi while we gloss over them, invisible

as they are to us. Though we've seen on TV—the satellite photos of *before* and *after* so that the river, normally a black seam in the center of the country, has ripped open, the whole fabric held together by fraying threads. But that's the aerial view, where metaphor comes easily. On the ground, the water rises with stubborn inevitability, or spills suddenly through strained levees. In either case, the end will be sodden carpets, sagging sofas, teacups with a residue of fine silt. Cats will cling to branches and hiss at their rescuers. For months, there will be the odor of mildew. If the structure is sound, they will pull the walls down and start over, this time with plasterboard. Inside, it will look almost as good as new, but it will be flimsier, flooded with the memory of water

cutting it down to size with its message of impermanence. Nothing lasts. Not childhood, nor your children's childhoods. Our fluid lives fall of their own gravity. So serious. How to show your child you love him. I'm fascinated that there could be people who would buy a book to tell how to do what ought to come naturally—or not at all. I try to imagine fifty-two different ways to show love, but I come up blank. I can't think of even one. Don't you show love by simply loving, whatever form it takes?

So, William will be waiting at the gate in Seattle and I'll take a minute to absorb him—still tall and thin, but in the two years since I've seen him, somehow more sure of himself, more settled into the angular face that nature handed him. On the way toward Olympia—William in front in his old Chevette, Stan and I behind in the rented car—he'll point off to our left and there it will be: Mt. Rainier pulling the sky around its massive shoulder. The sun will strike its highest peaks and wherever we turn the mountain will seem to be there, changing the landscape. And we will remember that when we were here once before, in January, we never saw it at all. Lost behind the weather of its own making.

How easily we slip from *there* to *here* in our thinking. Already, even before we've landed, the West Coast has become my reference point. I'll speak of my home in upstate New York as *there*, as in *in contrast to*. Because the *now* creates the *here*. For three weeks, *here* will refer to a rented house on a tiny island, joined to the peninsula by a concrete one-lane bridge. *Here* will mean the gradual flux of tides, the water lapping briefly at the foot of our deck or pulling back, revealing a spit of land where gulls line up single file for the sea's pickings. *Here* will also mean *now*

so that, when I call my father in Baltimore to tell him about this year's Perseid showers, he will be actively envious, although he's seen the Perseids almost every summer for eighty years. But this year they are different—closer to the earth than they have

85

been for two thousand years. This year, instead of lying on your back, staring at the unchanging sky until you think you could imagine a glimmer, a faint streak in the far corner, you will see them appear willy-nilly out of nowhere, making the darkness darker with their quick flare, their tracery of light. Over and over again, out over open water, a streak, an intake of breath. My father will miss them. He knows that they are there, invisible in the haze, the city's polluting light. *Now* is the year when, within this ancient cycle, the world measures time in centuries: twenty of them ago, when people looked up, how did they read these signs?

Four of us, two generations, lying on our backs on the deck. *There*, we will shout, and t*here*, but not one of us will see them all. We'll joke that Matthew and Robin will think the Perseids are always like this. Next year, and the next, they'll be disappointed. When they are old, they'll tell their grandchildren about tonight, carrying the tradition forward. In the East, the same bright streak—only three hours later on the clock. It's getting cold. Matthew wraps a quilt around Robin. They are easy together, affectionate. And under my pillow, the earth.

The human mind creates its world. Finds the baby Moses hanging upside down in the branches of Sitka spruce or madrona. The human heart pulls in the child and shares its mother-love. Stories unfurl as parable, metaphor for something larger—the myths that wind, like rivers, through our histories so that we call it culture—whatever it is that divides us. We study cultures—the way others think and act. Song, but not the urge to sing. Art, but not the need to paint. We search for difference when there is so much in common. Then we say they had it right, the aborigines, the elders, the ones who had a vision we have lost. The backward glance toward yesterday. But tomorrow offers up the sun. The world wants us. From above, we see it, parceled out in large rectangular fields that spread green or yellow from road to measured road, the isolated glint of farmhouse roof, or villages strung out in flight along the highway. Farther west, traces of the human are rare. Mountains push out of the ground in vast ripples of sunlight and shadow. Trees seem to flow over the ground. Water winks on and off as rivers reveal their wandering curves in reflections that shift like iridescent silk. From this angle, the land still waits for the likes of Lewis and Clark,

for man's penchant for numbers and maps. The world brought to its knees in longitude and latitude. Fixed points on a skittery surface. From above, you cannot tell when one country becomes another. Twelve years before Lewis and Clark, MacKenzie crossed the whole of Canada. The forty-ninth parallel was an arbitrary choice. And here comes history again, with its blunt snout pushing at the earth. The Pig War. A royal standoff between the armies of the United States and England, 1859–1872. Because an American farmer killed a boar belonging to the Hudson Bay Company on the Island of San Juan in the Straits of San Juan de Fuca, near Vancouver Island, somewhere below the forty-ninth parallel. The war was settled through arbitration by the kaiser, a cousin of Queen Victoria, who voted in favor of the United States. The only casualty was the pig. Change the maps, no one dies. The exception that proves the rule as though there were rules for war. Or rules in nature, for that matter. Order is a human need. Scott Russell Sanders, in "Earth's Body," uncovers it: "If I were to focus on the chirp of the snowy tree cricket . . . and if I were to count the number of beats in fifteen seconds, then add that number to thirty-seven, the sum would roughly equal the temperature in Fahrenheit." From this equation, however, Sanders moves rapidly to the cosmos, loafing and inviting his soul

but I am bound by something niggardly. My soul does not come when called. Instead of pondering the cricket, whose chirp slows or quickens depending on the weather, I think of the man behind the equation. Look what it takes just to set up the theorem: a clock, a numerical system, knowledge at what degree water will freeze, or boil. Then it takes some poor soul—some fool—to objectify his listening. When did he decide on the fraction of a minute? How did he arrive at the constant, thirty-seven? Unravel the equation and you move back into chaos—cacophony—save for some sense that sound is tethered to temperature. Sometime, maybe after generations of more generalized knowledge, some orderly mind measured the individual call of the individual cricket, refined and refined, through hours of trial and error, circling in on the variables until—*voilà!*—he reined them in and tied them with the rough equation. The universe doesn't give a damn about the glitter of numbers, their slippery trail down the page. The human mind, for whatever peculiar reasons, cares a great deal. What's foolish—or not so foolish—about the endeavor is the result. With clock and thermometer, altitude and algebra, we need not listen to the crickets to know whether or not to wear a jacket. But as a symbol of the way the world speaks to us and the way we talk back, now that's something else—

something that makes me think of how we deal with what we haven't understood. And the world requires understanding—why the tornados tossed in our path? Or take the slower form of disaster—rain, more rain, drop by drop, from Minnesota down through Iowa to where Missouri waits helplessly for the crest still weeks away?

Easy to let it recede. Out of sight, out of mind. We're there, or nearly here, as the engines grow loud and the plane begins its descent. The earth ticks. In the near future, my phone will ring and William Stafford will be dead. "Some time when the river is ice ask me / mistakes I have made. . . ." "Justice will take us millions of intricate moves. . . ." "Nothing is far anymore. . . ." "My self will be the plain / wise as winter is gray / pure as cold posts go / pacing toward what I know." I will wake in the morning and it will still be true and the words will persist. "Ask me whether / what I have done is my life."

Tomorrow I will wake in Matthew's home. I will look out his window and hear Western birds. On the weekend, we will drive the many miles over winding roads on Mt. Rainier to the lookout at Paradise. There we will walk out on subalpine meadows, covered with tiny purple and yellow flowers where, because of shadow and snowmelt, April often blooms alongside August. Matthew and Robin will spread out a blanket and we'll cut fruit and cheese, layers of sliced pork and avocado, whole wheat bread, cold tortellini. They will seem younger than I ever remember being, and yet they're both older than I was when I first held him in my arms, all wrinkled mouth and hiccup. I'm over fifty. I want to be their friend. Someone you'd like to have on a picnic in the rarefied air of a mountain, the sun a white glare on the glaciers and the stream December cold. What have I done with my life?

In 1972, after hurricane Agnes had found her way up the valley from Pennsylvania, then turned and followed the same path down again, they called it a "one-hundred-year flood." What did it matter how often it would come? Never again in my lifetime, was my mother's prayer. Never again her photographs, her best linen. When the water was gone, we tugged on our rubber gloves and pulled soggy handful after soggy handful of fiberglass insulation from between the studs. When we were done, the house was bare bones, my childhood peeled back to the lath, rough-hewn, and oddly exposed. The river swept on eastward to the Susquehanna, carrying with it its burden of memory. But that is the past, and somewhere in distant country

without fixed coordinates, tomorrow wanders. Looking for me, all future tense. High on a mountain, I will hear a sound I've never heard before—the whistle of a marmot. Bold. Unconsoled. As raw as grief. As unruly as love itself, which sweeps over me now as the giant wheels unfold from the well and the airplane shudders. Soon, in an ordinary moment that is mirrored at gate after gate in airport after airport, I'll walk through the door and William will wave.

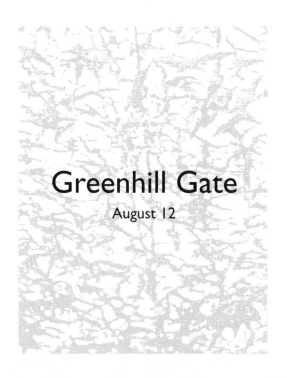

Greenhill Gate
August 12

We drive past without stopping—second gear up the steep incline, a flash of white gate, then downshift for the quick right and it's behind us. November, 1961: #2 Comely Bank, Edinburgh. Christina and I are making Thanksgiving dinner for some of our American friends. We've invited a few others from the Dramatic Society— Stephen Martineau, Andrew Kitchen, Neil Colombé. The oven is too small so we've spent hours trying to roast a turkey in the warming oven. No cranberries. No pumpkin pies. The meal is makeshift, but how would they know it doesn't meet traditional standards? Andrew is funny. I like him. He stalks the streets in his borrowed cape, his long hair. *All we can see now is the slate rooftop in the rearview mirror.* February, 1962: Edinburgh. Esmé, Andrew's mother, has come to visit him. Christina and I are making dinner for us all—beef stroganoff. This is the year we are learning to cook. We enjoy taking the string bag into shop after tiny shop—fishmonger's, chemist's, greengrocer's—returning with individually wrapped packets of soap, haddock, cereal, vinegar, carrots or plums. We buy milk in pint bottles, keeping them cool on the windowsill. Today, after classes, we spent the afternoon slicing meat, mushrooms and onions, curdling our homemade version of sour cream. "Andrew darling, do you remember the marsh birds on the Norfolk downs? They were spectacular, weren't they darling? This meal would be perfect for an evening like that—you could whip it up when the cook was off." *From below, it's no better; the trees at the edge of Greenhill Lane have grown so tall that the house is obscured.* April, 1962: Greenhill Gate, Bingley, Yorkshire. It's my first time at Andrew's home. We've hitchhiked up from Aberystwyth where our one-act was entered in the festival. We have no clean clothes because the suitcases, sent ahead by train, were delayed. I'm wearing the same wool skirt, sweater, knee socks I've worn for the last three days. Esmé excuses herself and when she returns she is wearing a long black dress, dark hair swept back, diamonds around her neck. Dinner is in the dining room. Stuffed salmon. Cream sauce. Fresh peas. Noel is gruff. He grumbles about business, about the drains in his fields, about America where, he tells me, he can't trust the people he works with. He comments that I bite my fingernails, as if I didn't already know. After dinner, there is coffee in the drawing room. The bedrooms are cold, each one opening off the long central hall that runs the length of the house. Mine is at the top of the back stairs. It used to be a maid's room. Now the help lives in an apartment in the converted barn. In the morning I will hear them come into the kitchen, the friendly chatter as they shine shoes, polish brass. I will go down the stairs and greet them as I make my way to the morning room. In the afternoon I will be told that, as a guest, I should not come down the back stairs. *There's no way to know the house is there except for the wall which must keep something in just as it keeps us out.* August, 1962: St. Pancras Town Hall, London. Andrew and I are getting married. It's clear that neither Esmé nor Noel would approve. We don't care. We have two secretaries for witnesses. They cry. We can't tell whether it's for our youth or the idea of marriage itself. Andrew buys me a white carnation. We walk all afternoon—first through Westminster Abbey, then the long miles to the station where he will take the train to Yorkshire. In October, in America, when we've told both sets of parents, Noel will write to us. "That's all right. I almost married a barmaid once myself." *The gate, with its intricate wrought iron hinges, is really a door to an interior world, a Secret Garden kind of gate.* 1948: Greenhill Gate. Andrew is eight. Leisa is five and Julie eleven. Noel Kitchen is their father now or, rather, Andrew's and Leisa's too—he's already Julie's father. He's bought the house on the hill. In the dining room, he's hung the painting of another house belonging to an earlier Kitchen in the North Riding of Yorkshire. With Greenhill Gate, he's restoring the family name. He doesn't pay much attention to an even earlier Kitchen who must have taken *his* name from a more lowly occupation. Before the war, Noel bought a hairpin factory. It was easy to convert it to retaining rings—those horseshoe-shaped pieces of metal that hold things together—necessary for motors, tanks, guns. *Open it and there's a walk leading up to the huge front door and then, beyond the patio, gardens—beds of roses, carefully planned perennials so there's always something in bloom, and behind them the kitchen garden with its gooseberries, Brussels sprouts, loose leaf lettuce.* Christmas Eve, 1963: Greenhill Gate. Esmé has called Andrew and Leisa and me to her upstairs bedroom. She is showering us with gifts. Too many. Too much. In one package, three nightgowns. "Judy darling, these are perfect for you." Downstairs, Noel sits in the drawing room alone. "I've told him I'll leave as soon as he buys me a house. Andrew dear, you have no idea how I've suffered. He's refused three perfectly good houses already. I know money doesn't buy happiness, but I'd like to be miserable in comfort." *And above the garden, the shortcut to the farm through dense woods filled with the harsh, eerie gossip of rooks.* August, 1964: Greenhill Gate. We're leaving for America. Suddenly it's time for the train—and the suitcases have been packed in the lavender Morris, not Noel's Jaguar. There's no room. We leave him standing at the gate. He waves once and turns back toward the house. *Molly must be in there now, one woman with all those rooms, all that space to echo her footsteps.* January, 1969: The Old Cottage, Farnham, Near Knaresborough, Yorkshire. We've come back across the ocean to stay in Esmé's new home and see Andrew's grandfather, bedridden in a nursing home. Handsome Bill Beard is no longer the dapper retired physician, son of a colonial judge, but a fragile eighty-year-old man, somewhat faded, more removed. He's glad we've come, glad when we leave. And so Andrew goes to Greenhill Gate. The fog is thick—it sticks to the hills and thins only slightly in the valleys where the sodium lights cast their odd orange circles on the pavement. Esmé is unhappy. "How can he go there? It's not as if he's his real father. Noel never liked him. He used to call him 'the professor.' How can he stand *her?*" *We could stop; I could introduce her to my new husband and we could sit stiffly in the drawing room trying to make conversation; we could listen to her aimless chatter and see that the house is only a house, after all.* June, 1974: Ocean View, Salcombe, Devon. Noel and Molly have decided to see us in their summer home. It's easier here, not so much that the children could break, not so many rules to remember. That doesn't make conversation easy, however. "Of course I sell to Franco's Spain. It's only the Germans I don't trust." "Your Andrew Young has no right to talk about South Africa. That's our business, not his." "I like hiring women—their fingers are thinner and they can do the work so much better, and I can pay them so much less." William and Matthew are young—they don't argue about such things. One afternoon their grandfather sneaks with them into the local hotel to play Ping-Pong. *But I am reluctant.* 1938 or 39: Esmé has come home from London to be married. She will begin her new life with a maid and a cook. When Andrew is born, she is given an infant's gas mask. They are sent to the country, where she can play the role of waiting wife. Her first husband will return from the war, but the marriage will be a casualty. *Why am I returning, like a voyeur, to the scenes of my past?* Summer, sometime: Greenhill Gate. Uncle Ian is practicing turning over his kayak in the canal.

Flip and he's under water, only his boat, like a long red finger, pointing toward the locks. Flip and he's upright, bald head shaking, water flying, paddles flashing. "Noel would have made a great feudal lord." Flip and he's disappeared again. *Maybe I don't want to surrender its hold on me.* June, 1979: The Old Cottage. Esmé does not want to come with us to Haworth. She's planning a party. A flurry of cooking and cleaning that is impossible to bear. I know I'm deserting, but I can't help it. In the triangular antique store at the top of the hill, I find a small blue porcelain dish in a pewter holder that exactly matches the one I bought my mother there five years ago. On the bottom is a tag that says "one of a set of three." One to go. And when we get back, we are slightly annoyed at the bother and fuss, the way nothing is exactly right and we can't make it better. *Maybe I want to put something to rest.* December, 1979: After his mother's funeral, Andrew meets a man called Godfrey Lupton Whitelock. His biological father. "What was it like?" "It was like meeting a rather pleasant man. Nothing else." *For twenty-four years, this was the house where I could never belong.* Ask Leisa. Ask Julie. Did anyone ever belong? *Now Stan and I drive by, up to the public footpath where the walk over Ilkley Moor begins.* Winter, 1984: Greenhill Gate. I am no longer a part of this life and so I can only imagine them gathered around the fire noting, for the first time, how easy it is to speak without Noel's stiff presence to tie the tongue. He came in from gardening to make a business call. Five minutes later, Molly found him, seated in his favorite chair, not a hair out of place. *It only takes a couple of hours, perfectly straight on the trace of an old Roman road, past stone circles, origin unknown, and then down into the market town of Ilkley.* The family goes on, like a soap opera that has lost its two main characters. *From there, you can take the bus back, through the populous valley, circling a land that is wild and remote, gruff in the wind, belonging to no one.*

Not Less Because
Ways of Looking
at Wallace Stevens

I was the world in which I walked, and what I saw

when I came down the stairs, dressed for the party as Little Red Riding Hood, was my Aunt Margaret in shorts and a tunic with a quiver on her back. She was Robin Hood—her hair pulled back and piled on her head so it would fit beneath the green felt cap. The scar on her cheek, suddenly so exposed, seemed almost a part of the disguise. I could almost hear the clank of swords, see the thrust and jab, the quick slash, blood. Oh, I knew it really came from falling, as an infant, onto the hot air register—an angry cross burned into her cheek, fading over the years to something that gave her face its dignity. But this was a dress-up world and any minute the wolf would discover me and open his wide mouth. I'd be swallowed, lost inside a speechless shell, like Johnny Harr who was gassed in World War I and came home to live with his brother, a timid man with something inside trying to escape through his damaged vocal cords and restless fingers. Once he touched my cheek, and it burned for days. So

Nothing is lost, loud locusts. No note fails

to hold remembered sound. It all comes back in black and white. In muted color, from a sable brush. Pink roses climb the trellis to my window. Faint scent, and yellow hum. And in the evening, through the screens, the moiré patterns shimmer on the lawn. Downstairs,

the music
Will be motion and full of shadows

and the shadows will be dancing on the walls. The music will come from the corner where a scratchy phonograph is piled with a stack of 78s. As they thunk down onto each other, the stack will rise, beginning to wobble so the sound will be warped. The dancers will wash past, all moving lips and teeth beneath their masks. There is only the dance—half-moon, an archer's bow, motion spun of shadow, frenzied light—but

The dance has no name. It is a hungry dance.

It is the dance of winter kites, caught in the tips of trees. It tugs and trails a useless string. It holds more than a lifetime of memory

And when the cock crows on the left and all

my mother's stories come to life, I'm on the farm where she grew up. I see the hens in a frantic pecking at her feet. Her gentle horse, all quivering mouth and snicker of hot breath on the sugared hand. The watering trough which, in deep summer, defines dream—mossy cool, secret, serene. Most of all, I see her climb the ladder to the hayloft where, from her perch, she can watch the slant of sunlight catch the floating chaff, lifting it lazily through the heat like gauze, a curtain of shifting light. A summer smell, dry as tinder, sweet. And the rooster, voracious, like a prancing jester, who can only

Play the present, its hoo-hoo-hoo.

The present is a vivid past. It was April, the month before I learned to read. I was sitting in the apricot tree. Around me, petals fell like snow. I was wearing my red and white striped overalls. Words were simply sound. They made a presence in the April air.

It is April as I write. The wind

comes up at night. In the morning, nothing has changed. If we wake early, we hear the bark of straggler geese—faint cry filtered through cloud. Spring is late. Snowdrops on the lawn, and the tattered skirt of snow at its edges, preserved in shadow. This is a season of indecision. The mind breaks formation, heads north into deeper silence.

Silence is a shape that has passed

but not before the shape has been noted and held in the mind so the hands can reproduce it. It is absence of cricket, lull in birdsong as morning brightens, cessation of the incessant bleeping (like a blinking traffic light) of the garbage truck. The mind knows silence in the midst of sound. It is round. Smooth. A stone worn by water. Porcelain cup. Cylinder of ice. Thought, before words, lifting from its branch on sculpted wings as

If thinking could be blown away

like a leaf. And if it could, I would lose it in a lacquered sky. All predicate and noun, twisted into a helix of meaning. I would not now be thinking of my Uncle Willy.

It was his nature to suppose

and so he spent his time supposing. His thoughts churned—
and he had time to let them churn as he sat all day in his nurs-
ing-home room, a room almost as stripped of character as his
apartment had been. What he was was all inside. There were no
colorful Mexican serapes or Egyptian footstools to testify to
travel. In fact, he hardly traveled, except to see his sister or brother
in the east. And there he spent his days stretched on the couch or
at the kitchen table, a book in hand, a beer handy. He did not go
far and, when he spoke, he spoke fitfully. His silences were punctuated with snorts—private laughter, internal amusement. Then
he'd begin one of his "supposings" and out would come fully
formed argument, usually on something one would never think
to argue about. They were amusing, inconsequential little spurts
of logic, applied to the inanities of the day. They made a limited
kind of sense, but today I am forced to admire the larger logic of
which they were a part. In the wake of an amputation and a stroke,
he has refused to eat. He clenches his fingers to make a fist and
declares that

Death is absolute and without memorial.

Its finality is infinite. Honor his choice—for that is what it is:
his last living testament to the imagination. He clenches his fingers to make a fist.

Let be be finale of seem.

The rest is all conditional. We step in and out of the past,
project a future, a future perfect. In it, my mother will climb
down the ladder and put another record on the spindle. The dancers will have been waltzing below me. One, two, three / you and
me / where to now / why and how / life could be/ if only . . .

If the day writhes, it is not with revelations

but with sunlight and shadow, with one question asking itself over and over. The meticulous clock, unsprung, spits out its seconds one by one. Who will miss him when he's gone, when silence spreads out its colored beads and the hand lifts each of them gently and holds it to the light?

Dark things without a double, after all

are doubly dark—so truly dark they cast no shadow. Dark the way the bottom of a cistern is dark. A stone dropped is hiatus and then a faint echo and the echo is a hole between stars. The shutter opens inside the camera's case. If there were an opposing value, it would not be light, but weightlessness. Hammers would float. The body would somersault in dazzling space. Yes,

The imperfect is our paradise

and that is where we find ourselves. We spend the days, working and re-working, hammering home our bent language. How we love our missed connections. How we adore what we have yet to say. We spin in ecstatic disarray, unpin our hair, dance in our bodies—our body's delight. How perfect we are in our imperfections. How suddenly we love our worldly weight.

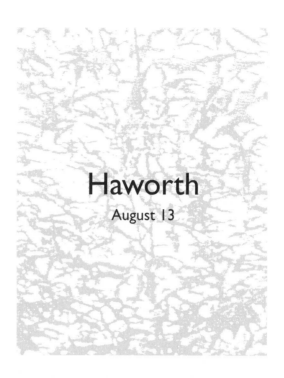

Haworth
August 13

Nothing has changed here. Not since I first came. Not since the Brontës themselves walked these streets. Well, of course that's an exaggeration. Today there are hundreds of tourists pulling themselves up the steep cobblestoned streets. First a tour of the house where they all grew up—three inventive sisters and a brilliant, sickly brother; then the church where the father presided; after that, according to age or disposition, a walk on out onto the moors or else a spot of tea in town, a quick look round for Yorkshire biscuits or clover honey.

But what a wonder that they have come. This summer, following the Gulf War, tourism is at its all-time low. Air fares, oil prices, the threat of terrorism, who knows? But the British love their authors, whose lives are as real to them as those of Elvis or Marilyn are to us. Here, in the remote West Riding of Yorkshire, time flows backward.

Two miles below, the industrial town of Keighley still belches smoke into the atmosphere. Factory after factory, narrow streets huddled along the trough of the Leeds-Liverpool canal, grey stone row houses struggling up the hillsides until they peter out at the pasture's edge. After that, a few dilapidated farms and then rough, uncontainable moorland. Up here, the houses defend themselves against the wind. They rise up lonely. Lovely in their resilience. The sky widens and descends. Wall and tree, even tufts of grass, make silhouettes against its changing landscape.

Up here, Catherine and Heathcliff meet at Top Withens. They are as real as the cold, stone parsonage, the dark, hard-hearted church. As real as the gravestones laid end to end like paving stones in the churchyard.

It's a ten-mile hike to Top Withens, over moorland so wild that heather grows tough and wily as the sheep. And when you get there, you're not quite sure you've arrived. Some ruins, yes, but then there are other ruins, and any of them might do. So it's the getting there that counts because the walk is hard and the imagination untethers itself, raw and ravenous.

So you return to the tiny town, perched on the edge of the century. Outside your window, in liquid light, the local players begin their game of cricket. Busloads of tourists head downhill. Soon you will be left with the faint *pock* of ball on bat, the curlew's watery cry, and a scent of smoke that clings to your hair and clothes like a reminder.

Tomorrow, if you go back the way you came, you will enter the world quickly with a shock of recognition. There will be traffic and news reports and lunch in the pub. But if you head out on the small roads that progress has forgotten, you will wind down the backs of the hills toward Burnley and the Motorway. On the way, you will need to stop as cattle lumber down the road, driven by a young man who might, once, have inhabited a novel. They will brush past your car, so close you need to roll up the windows against the flies. They come in a steady stream, part briefly, then flow together again in the rearview mirror. Their faces are slow and placid. They know nothing but this path toward pasture. They carry the sun on their backs. They are bedrock. Going. Gone.

Lillian Pendell, age two and a half

Lillian as a girl,
circa 1919

Lillian Pendell, 1930
("Lily")

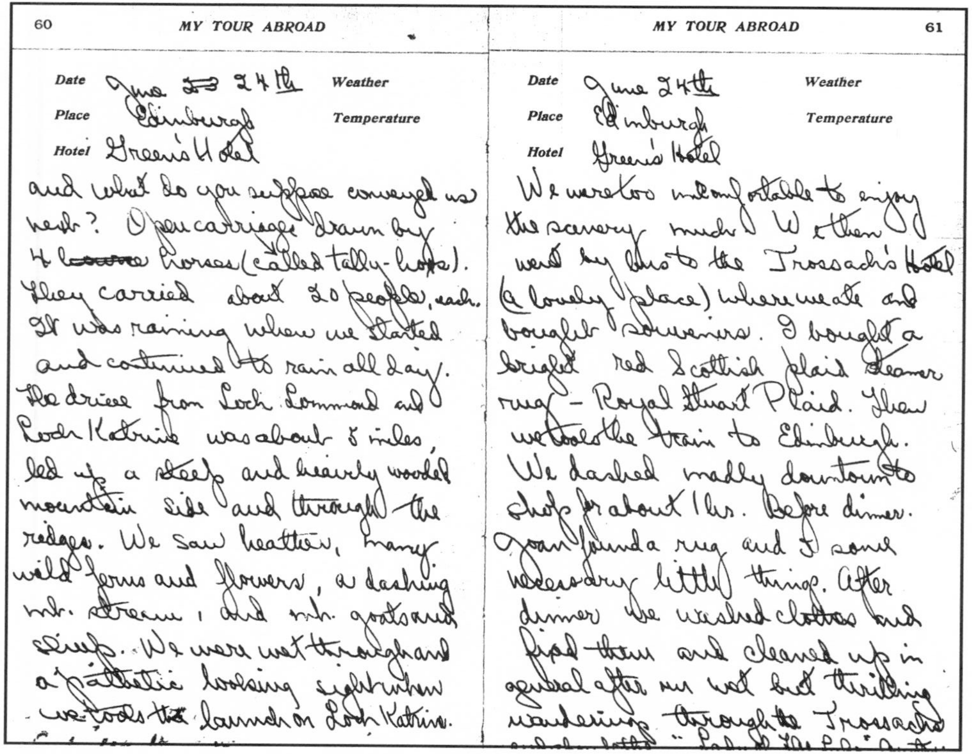

60 MY TOUR ABROAD

Date June ~~23~~ 24th Weather
Place Edinburgh Temperature
Hotel Green's Hotel

and what do you suppose conveyed us
next? Open carriage drawn by
4 ~~horses~~ horses (called tally-hops).
They carried about 20 people, each.
It was raining when we started
and continued to rain all day.
The drive from Loch Lommond and
Loch Katrine was about 5 miles,
led up a steep and heavily wooded
mountain side and through the
ridges. We saw heather, many
wild ferns and flowers, a dashing
mt. stream, and mt. goats and
sheep. We were wet through and
a pathetic looking sight when
we took ~~the~~ launch on Loch Katrine.

MY TOUR ABROAD 61

Date June 24th Weather
Place Edinburgh Temperature
Hotel Green's Hotel

We were too uncomfortable to enjoy
the scenery much. We then
went by bus to the Trossach's Hotel
(a lovely place) where we ate and
bought souvenirs. I bought a
bright red Scottish plaid steamer
rug – Royal Stuart Plaid. Then
we took the train to Edinburgh.
We dashed madly downtown to
shop for about 1 hr. before dinner.
Joan found a rug and I some
necessary little things. After
dinner we washed clothes and
hung them and cleaned up in
general after our wet but thrilling
wandering through the Trossachs

Excerpt, Lillian's European diary, 1930

Lillian and Judy, 1944

Bob and Lillian,
Workshop Players,
circa 1945

Margaret Randels,
costume party, 1945

Bob, George, and Judy, with rabbit, 1946

On the woodpile, 1946

Margaret and Ray, wedding on the lawn, 1948

George and Judy at Aunt
Margaret's wedding, 1948

Margaret Randels Warner,
1949

Palm trees,
Rio de Janeiro

William and
Matthew,
Jardim Botanico,
Rio de Janeiro,
1971

Ten Stories

Tonight I am sitting in the elegant dining room of an old Victorian hotel on the shores of Lake Chautauqua in western New York State. The huge fans on the high ceiling circle above the whirling conversations of the guests. Young men and women weave among the white-clothed tables carrying trays of food. Each table is assigned to a long-term guest, and we are here in someone's place. "Mr. and Mrs. Charles Gordon" are dining on the veranda this evening, and so we transients are allowed a table. Our waitress is Kelly. She is about twenty, earnest and friendly. At the end of the season, she will wait anxiously for her tip from Mr. and Mrs. Gordon. Our tip has been carefully built into the price of the meal.

Look around the room. Except for the fashions, it might as well be 1927 in Wequetonsing in Michigan, where the young woman was named Lillian. She was working her way through college and her friendly manner and careful attention to detail made her a popular waitress. Her tips meant the difference between scrimping and a little pleasure.

Lillian bobbed her dark hair in the style of the day, parted on the right. Given a different life, she could have been dancing in the nightclubs of New York City. Occasionally, when her face relaxed, she was beautiful. But when she was working, her forehead was knitted with the effort of getting everything right. She was purposeful and practical. And so she refused the nickname Lily, just as she hated the photograph that captured the other, softer self—the one where a slight smile plays across her face and the neckline of her dress makes a V that suggests a not-quite-repressed sensuality.

In the next few years Lillian would complete college and begin teaching Latin in a school in central Michigan. She would travel a bit—once to the Southwest where she bought a turquoise and silver bracelet, once to Europe where she posed for snapshots that seem, at least to her children, wildly free. She would marry a young math teacher and then work to help him finish graduate school in physics. Eventually, at the age of thirty-three, she would become my mother.

Who was she? Do we ever really know our mothers? For some, I suspect, the answer must be yes. Their mothers talk to them, person to person. I don't think my mother did that. Even in our later years, she spoke about people we had in common, mutual worries, my brother's divorce, my children's latest antics, but not about herself. Nothing intimate. And so I piece her together like a puzzle, but it's an old puzzle and many of the pieces are missing. When you are finished, you have to imagine the missing piece, the way it would fill with color and shape and make the picture whole. And there are places where several contiguous pieces are gone and, even though there might be a bird or a tree in the picture, you will never know it because there is not even a clue.

That's the way it is when I think of my mother. She becomes a series of stories, discrete and possibly directionless. Sometimes I miss her terribly, thinking that only she would care what is happening to me, her fifty-year-old child. And sometimes she intrudes—an attitude, a tightening of the lips. Or she becomes a feeling—no, two separate feelings. With one, I am needy. I beg. With the other, I muster every defense I have to fend her off.

A therapist might say (my old friend Christina might say) that I need to come to terms with her. But I think not. I look at the Lillian on my wall—the picture she hated most—and that's the woman I want to know. I wish I could be that beautiful, that aloof.

Who was she? I know the story of her life. I know she grew up on a farm, in poverty, walking miles to school each day. I know how hard she worked. I know her mother, my grandmother Mayme, and how hard *she* worked. I know my mother did not have new clothes and time for dreaming. I know that she wore braces on her teeth—a sacrifice unheard of in those times. I know that she worked her way through high school, and college, and graduate school, pulling around her the identity of schoolteacher for the rest of her life. I know the facts, but I don't know her.

She was my Girl Scout leader and my Latin teacher. She cooked my meals and called me in for bed. She put the labeled baby food jars in a line on the shelf and gave me my quarter allowance in nickels, one in each jar: Xmas Gifts, Green War Saving Stamps, Church, Savings, Spending Money. She lived, and died, outside of me. I do not feel her life the way I feel the lives of my sons. Sometimes I am guilty, thinking that I *should*, that any good daughter *should*.

Story #1: I am standing at the sink, washing dishes, when the sound happens. Something different that shakes the air. It takes a while to register because for years now we have been so used to the sound of the trains, at regular intervals, slowing slightly for the crossing and then streaming off into the distance with the faint whine of a diesel horn. This time, however, the train seems to shudder and we can hear the whoosh of braking. "Oh my god," says my mother, rushing for the front door. I pull my hands from the suds and run for the back door, taking the short cut through the yard. By the time I arrive, the train has stopped and I can see the twisted wreckage of the car, an older man and a young woman standing dazed at the side of the tracks, an old woman lying at the edge of the tracks, perfect in her stillness. It does not occur to me that she could be dead. There is no blood.

I pick my way carefully toward the crossing and then I see the local doctor scrambling into the ditch at the bottom of the embankment. There's another woman down there, covered with blood, writhing in pain. "I need help," he calls, and then my mother steps out from the gathering crowd, crawls down to him and holds the woman's neck exactly where he tells her to. For what seems like hours, they work together, waiting for the ambulance. After the woman has been taken to the hospital, my mother washes herself and makes a cup of coffee. Then she calls to offer her house to the woman's husband and daughter who must wait in a strange town while she is cared for. The woman's sister is dead and the woman will take ten long days to die also. Meanwhile two strangers live in our house. I have forgotten their names.

I have forgotten almost everything except my mother's calm manner as she tears her slip into strips and works over the woman, the way the doctor speaks, and then the way my mother, without flinching, puts pressure on the place to make the bleeding stop.

Story #2: My cousin Tommy is three when he comes to stay with us for a week. Tommy is considered to be a "handful," and my mother secretly suspects that my Aunt Margaret has not been tough enough. The first morning Tommy has oatmeal for breakfast. He asks for more. When she dishes it out, he says he's full.

For the next three meals, my mother puts a bowl of cold oatmeal at Tommy's place. She is determined to make him eat what he has asked for. To give him his due, he's got a stubborn streak. He refuses to eat. My brother George and I watch this drama in awe. It had never occurred to us that we could take so definitive a stand. When will he give in? We imagine the oatmeal, more congealed with each meal, cold and slimy and old. We imagine the first bite, the way the throat will convulse and the stomach turn. We imagine the way he will eventually get used to it, even take pride in the way he can wolf it down.

But for three meals that doesn't happen. We begin to imagine Tommy at the end of the week, weak and disoriented, staggering toward his mother who has come to retrieve him. We imagine his ribs sticking out and his stomach swollen. We imagine him docile and defeated. The fourth meal, my mother simply hands Tommy a peanut butter and jelly sandwich and life goes on. The oatmeal has been surreptitiously scooped into the garbage. It's over.

Story #3: My mother's the director and my father has a part in the play. The Workshop Players put on lots of plays, using the small stage on the top floor of the Corning Public Library. This involves rehearsals and productions, props and prompts, and endless stories after the fact. Parties for the cast. Selection of the next productions. This evening there's excitement in the air. My father is putting on his costume, snapping his black suspenders and slicking his red hair back in an earlier style, trying on a pair of wire-rimmed glasses. My mother is laughing.

Story #4: My mother is telling us tongue twisters. She never gets tired of "Theophilus Thistle the Successful Thistle Sifter," which she says very fast. For years, we thought of it as "the awfulest thistle." Then she lisps into "Thome people are interethted in one thing, thome people are interethted in other thingth, but I'm motht interethted in thpitting. I can thpit in long lineth and thort lineth and in thircleth and thpiralth and puddleth. One day I met a man on the thtreet. He thaid, 'Would you thpit for me?' And tho I did. I thpat both marvelouthly and quickly. I thpat tho well I thocked him right between the eyeth. He wath both thurprithed and pleathed. But I think he wath more thurprithed than pleathed."

Story #5: I want a new dress for the dance. What I want, of course, is to be tall and beautiful and somewhat reserved. Since that's not possible, I want a dress that will make me feel that way. I know I don't need a dress—I have two in the closet and each has been worn twice. But this dance is different, and I want to look the way I think the other girls looked the last time, and I want a different corsage—not just carnations or tiny rosebuds but a gardenia. I want its pungent odor next to my skin; I want the way it turns brown if you touch it. I want to be sophisticated and untouchable just about exactly as much as I want to whisper and tumble and touch. The two feelings do not go together, and I suspect that a dress might tie my feelings in a package and tell me how to think and act. A dress will make a difference.

My mother does not see the necessity for a dress. I've spent my clothes allowance and I should learn how to live within a budget. She has been saving her own money for a cherry coffee table. I should have saved mine.

The new dress is pink. It's not my best color, yet the cut of the dress and the flare of the skirt, the way it comes off the shoulder without being a stupid strapless gown—everything about it is just right. Of course I don't have the right shoes, or anything else, but at least I have the dress. When I come down the stairs, my mother tells me that I am wearing her cherry coffee table.

Story #6: My son William has left *blay* somewhere and he is inconsolable. *Blay* is his blanket—by now a grey strip of thin cotton cloth, what anyone who found it would call a rag and throw away. William wants *blay*, with whom he talks and pretends. My mother walks back through the village, retracing every step they have taken this morning. She comes back triumphant, waving a filthy *blay* that she found stuffed into the mouth of a cannon in the park. She tucks it into William's hand and leads him upstairs for his nap.

I am busy taking care of Matthew, who is two weeks old. My mother has made William her special charge. She understands what it is to be two and to have a new brother. She was an only child and so she understands in ways that I do not. I think William should get used to it.

Story #7: My mother is cutting the cake—her special chocolate cake, with chocolate frosting which she cooks in a Pyrex double boiler on the top of the stove, the mixer whirring until the icing begins to form peaks. Each piece looks exactly like the next. Until, that is, she decides which one of us gets the first choice. George looks them over, trying to size up his advantage, examining each piece for the most icing, the fraction of an inch greater height or width. I am sick with envy. It should be my turn. At least that's the way I remember it. He's been first two times in a row. It's not fair.

I wonder, now, why she didn't simply put a plate in front of each of us, letting our eyes fill with chocolate frosting. Who would have noticed the infinitesimal differences? Can jealousy be taught? Refined?

Story #8: Yesterday I fell while skinning the cat on my closet bar. My mother heard the crash and heard me crying. She offered me some gum drops—that's what she does when we hurt ourselves. But I didn't stop crying, all day long. So when my father came home, he drove me into town for an X-ray, and now I have a white sling to hold my arm close to my body so it won't hurt any more. But this morning I can't walk into the kitchen for my breakfast. I know it sounds silly. Even at four I can see that it doesn't make sense. But every time I leave the couch and walk through the dining room toward the cheerful kitchen, with its blue table set with my cereal, I come to a particular floorboard in the dining room and feel a stab of pain. If I step back, it goes away. Truly, I understand why she doesn't believe me, but I want her to. If I think hard enough, even now, I can feel that hot knife in my right shoulder, enough to make me step back to catch my breath. Enough to make me desperate for the Wheaties which she will not, under any circumstance, bring on a tray to the couch.

Story #9: My mother and I are giving a surprise birthday party for Pat, who has been living with us for the year. Pat, we are sure, has never had a real birthday party. She is one of twelve children and she is living with us because her mother kicked her out of the house when she reached sixteen. But Pat is different from her sisters. She didn't head for the nearest bar or throw herself on the first trucker who claimed to be single. She is going to finish high school and become something. When I asked my mother if Pat could live with us, it did not take her long to fix up the extra room.

The year with Pat, my mother and I didn't fight. We didn't want her to see us fight and so we both made efforts. And now ten girls from the senior class are waiting in our living room, ready to shout *surprise* when Pat comes through the door. My mother is almost giddy with anticipation, as though the party were for her.

Story #10: I don't like to visit the Harrs because their house smells dark and moldy, a stench of age and loneliness. And Johnny Harr is scary. He tries to talk and his hands wave wildly as his mouth twists round and round its awful, wailing sounds. My mother says he was injured in the first war and that he's come home to live with his brother and his wife. My mother goes to visit at least once a week, pushing George in his three-wheeled buggy and holding me by the hand. When we get there, Mrs. Harr tickles George under the chin and tries to get me to sit on her lap, but I pull away. I keep watching Johnny, who scares me. He is more frightening than the wolf in "The Three Little Pigs," and sometimes I feel as though my own house has blown down. I want to run out into the fields of corn where I can hide in the dizzying rows until I think I may never come out. Or on, into the pasture, where black-eyed Susans and Queen Anne's lace wave in the wind. Or on further, into the woods where we sometimes walk, looking for pink lady-slippers or jack-in-the-pulpits. Where we pick the wintergreen leaves and chew them, letting them slowly become fibrous pulp in our puckered mouths. I want to run away from my mother and her kindness. I never want to hear Johnny Harr's sounds again. They come from somewhere in myself—a place so lost you can never find it, a place that little girls should never know.

Story without end: At seventy-two, my mother is dying. She has been dying for several years, but now it's clear to anyone who sees her. Her body is too thin. Her hair has grown back, but thin and wispy. Her broken arm, the one that will never mend, is held together by a pin and is carefully encased in a specially designed sling. She is dying of metastasized breast cancer, a cancer gone to the bone—seven years of pain and fruitless treatment. By the time it was fully diagnosed, she was already too weak to go through a rigorous chemotherapy. And so everything was done in small doses, a half-hearted pretense at containment. Nothing that could "cure."

It would have been different if she had talked about it. At least that's what I thought then. If we had taken the opportunity to sort out our lives—her place in mine, my place in hers. If we had done what the knowledge of death allows you to do.

Sometimes I envy those who lose someone to accident: the surprise, the sharp stab of pain, the grief. It's hard to grieve what you know is coming, what you watch month after painful month, what you cannot speak aloud. It's hard to feel anything but the guilt of relief, and that is a guilt that does not, somehow, recede. You know it's normal—even necessary—but you'd like to feel something larger. You'd like to give her life its proper place in your heart.

Two weeks before her death, my mother, with my father's assistance, got out her bowls and her mixer and laboriously measured out the ingredients for a poppy-seed cake. When it was done, she put on her best yellow dress and rode with him to Addison, taking the cake to the school librarian, Audrey Cloos, who had married the art teacher, Norman Phelps. She sat in the front seat while my father delivered the cake, and when Audrey and Norman came out to thank her, she nodded and smiled and was wholly herself.

In the outside world, Ronald Reagan was running for president. Inside her house, my mother was dying. I had come home for the weekend and the doctor had dropped by for his regular evening "visit," then called my father and me into the study. Did we want her here or in the hospital? We made the wrong decision, but we didn't know at the time that it was wrong. We decided to let her stay at home where everything was familiar. And so we began the long, slow process of watching her starve to death. Six days of drifting between shots of morphine. Six days of family—each with a different idea of how to grieve the dying, the dead. Our nerves grew taut and always, always in the bedroom, the constant clock of her breathing. The way it wouldn't stop.

My mother was dying and she never talked to me. She never once said she was dying—in fact, she talked always of when she would be better—and so the denial went on. People called her brave, even heroic. *Your wonderful mother*, the neighbors said. *Your incredible mother*, her friends all told me. My mother, who withheld, even at the end, what she might have given me: a chance to say *thank you*, and *let's let bygones*, and *why?* The opportunity that death, once you know it is coming, holds out to you. Take this, it says, it's your last chance. You can look at your whole life now, and see its shape. You can say what you've done, and what you still wanted to do. You can sit down with the daughter who caused you grief and tell her that things have worked out, after all. You can let her know that you are not so disappointed. You can go over a lifetime—the day she was born, the day she broke her collarbone, the day she invited herself to a birthday party and both you and the other mother had to pretend it was true. You can remind her of the time it rained for three days and three nights when you were camping with the Girl Scouts. Or the time she ran away as far as the cemetery and came home scared before you'd even discovered she was missing. You can tell her how much you love her teenage sons, how glad you have been to see them grow. How much you will miss them. You can move forward together, planning their futures, although you both know they will probably never do what you plan. And you can move backwards, to the young woman framed on her wall—Lily—whose dreams you can't recall, and to the Lillian you remember well in her sturdy shoes and starched uniform. You can tell your daughter about that summer waiting on tables, how, in your free hours in the early afternoon, you tried to learn to swim, swallowing your fear and screaming with delight as the tanned young waiters tossed you into shallow water. You can tell her, again, about the watering trough on the farm. When you were little, you would slip into it, letting your body rise slowly, amazed at its casual buoyancy.

White Roads
The Landscape
of Leslie Norris
Wales, August 15

We are lost again. The road has narrowed to one lane and tilted upward, heading straight for the sky. There's no going back, but it's clear that this is not the A40 out of Brecon toward Llandovery. The stone walls hem us in, then suddenly give way to open moorland. For miles, stretching in front of us, nothing but bracken and heather and sheep and a sense that just over the rim there is more of the same. It's early evening and the light is remarkable—grey and more grey, with the occasional shaft of sunlight that gives us the land piecemeal. This is new terrain—lovely and lonely. The wind makes the only sound.

We are lost and, although light loiters on a Welsh summer evening, these hills seem to soak it up. Dusk, and we have a hotel waiting. A hotel on a road the map shows in green—the A40 through Trecastle. And this road, barely one lane, is not even a yellow road that clearly goes from one place to another. No, this must be another white road, those lines you can hardly follow on the map, meeting at unmarked crossroads, known only to those who know where they're going. Hold the map at arm's length and those roads disappear altogether.

Giddy with lack of direction, one is tempted by the ridiculous. I roll down the window to ask the nearest sheep. Our laughter is lost in the wind. And then we see him. He's an old man, wearing a sweater and cap, long white hair, a walking stick, someone who belongs. His stride is sure. His answer is less certain—we really can't get there from here. Or, yes, we can, if we go back to the cattlegrid, turn left and open the gate, follow the roads always downward, toward the A40 which we will eventually hit not all that far from Trecastle. So when we come to the gate we feel free to open it, to enter what looks so much like someone's private territory, and we descend, twisting past tiny farms, little white-washed cottages tucked into the hillside, hedgerow windbreaks, small closed farmyards with a clutter of sheds, the isolated barking of a suspicious dog.

When my great-grandfather came out of the hills above Llandovery in 1864, his furniture on a flat cart, his pans in clanking bundles, his pots in wicker baskets, his two small boys kicking their legs over the backboard, you can be sure he brought his dogs with him. He was not migrating very far—not more than fifty miles—but he was leaving behind the green, Welsh-speaking country in which he had been born. He never went back. He walked with his wife at the mare's head through the hamlets of Halfway and Llwel, and his cousins the Gardners ran out to wish them luck and to give them parting gifts—small lustre jugs, packets of tea. Reaching Sennybridge, they turned south to climb the gaunt and steering heights of the Brecon Beacons.

The Castle Hotel (one of several with this name within the Sennybridge phone exchange) turns out to be one of the three pubs in Trecastle. The rest of the village consists of a store and a sprinkling of houses. The inn has a formal dining room—lace tablecloths, flowers—but we choose the pub where the people are. The girl behind the bar switches easily from English to Welsh, depending on the customer. She tells us she's from a nearby farm, one we probably passed as we wound our way down into town. There's a man who has lived here for eighteen years; he refers to himself as a "Yorkshireman." The food is fantastic—lamb with roast potatoes, carrots, salad with avocado and shrimp. We're warm and safe and somewhere above us there is moorland, so green it is black.

At exactly 9:30 an old man enters the pub. The girl pulls a glass off the shelf and pours a whiskey. It's ready even before he descends the first step. Another customer quickly—almost guiltily—removes his coat from the back of the chair by the fire. That, it turns out, is Ted's chair. He shuffles toward it, sits, his back painfully straight as he stares ahead, speaking to no one. Occasionally he takes a sip. "You can set your watch by him," someone says.

The next morning we set out, deliberately taking the white roads over Black Mountain, the long way to Merthyr Tydfil. In fifteen hundred miles, we have seen nothing so desolate. The roads drop off into fog. On one side, sheer rock face; on the other, a falling away—a falling without end since whatever is there is simply swallowed in mist. Grey and more grey and then we are descending and the morning sun is burning off the fog and it seems there is nothing so charming as each isolated cottage. Soon we see the terraced streets of the city.

Here the little boys climbed down to lighten the load as, dwarfed by height, silenced by darkness, the family crawled for hours under black Fan Frynach before they reached the top of the pass at the Storey Arms Inn. Then they could see below them the spoiled valleys of Glamorgan, their sides already pocked with the heaped detritus of the Industrial Revolution, their skies lit by leaping flames from the furnaces or hidden by rolling smoke.

The Castle School Museum in Merthyr Tydfil tells us the history. The Dowlais iron works were founded here in 1759 and

thus a tiny Welsh village was transformed. By 1801, Merthyr
Tydfil had a population of nearly 8,000, overtaking Swansea as
the largest town in Wales. In 1851 there were 46,000 people,
many of whom lived in squalor. It was here that Trevithick demonstrated the first locomotive to run under its own steam. As the
ironworks shut down in the last half of the nineteenth century,
Merthyr switched to coal mining. In 1900, the city elected Keir
Hardie to Parliament as Britain's first Labour MP. The city suffered during the Great Depression—at one time, 50 percent of
its citizens were out of work—and at the end of the decade many
of its young men fought, and died, in the Spanish Civil War.
This is the heart of Welsh memory—work and more work until
one day there is no work and even the revolution is too late.

> . . . *He was not going to the foundries or the coal mines but
> to a farm on the clear hills above the newly smoking town. He
> would have a white house, thick-walled, four-square to the
> winds; he would have an enclosure of over forty acres and
> grazing rights on twelve long miles of open mountain. On those
> high, unhindered moors he would raise his sheep—not your
> demure symbols of meekness, all soft fleece and gentle bleating,
> but stubborn, short-tempered animals, malevolent and cun-
> ning, able to grow stout on the shortest grass, yellow-eyed as
> goats, fluent as goats on the rock faces.*

That afternoon, in Brecon, a man comes up to us in the bookstore. He is handsome in his wool sweater, tweed cap. "Did you
find your way?" he asks, and it takes us a minute to see that this is
the same man from whom we asked directions on the moors. He
is out of place here in the bookshop. To us, he is frozen on the
moors—a man without a life except as we give it to him in our
story. It comes as a shock that people *live* here. They walk down
the hillsides and into town. They read; they listen to jazz. This is
what it is, then, to be a tourist. You come and then go, taking
with you anecdote, reference, but nothing of the actual living.
You swallow the history in small bites, spitting out the seeds. You
take only what you want. You have that luxury.

117

What if you grew up here? What if you couldn't drive on, brushing off the crumbs? What if it stayed inside you, indelible, haunting in its green-black density? What if your own history *was* the history of the land? Would you carry it with you wherever you went? Would it rise in you somewhere in Hampshire or Utah and find its way onto the page? *I'm glad I had my boyhood before the war, before the '39 war, that is. I'm glad I knew the world when it was innocent and golden and that I grew up in a tiny country whose borders had been trampled over so often that they had been meaningless for centuries.*

The writer goes back to what formed him, to the child for whom external landscape and internal voice are one and the same. To the child who enters language not only with words for *mother* or *father*, but with words for *sky* and *hill* and *beyond*. To that child, the view will always be foreshortened; the light will play across valleys, fickle as love itself, and the sky will offer its one syllable endlessly, promising, promising.

The reader is a tourist, and the tourist is the incurable romantic. So we enter the text, following the white roads. We enter his childhood through the *fact* of our own. *I tried to tell him that I liked getting to school early, that I liked being alone on the playground when it was silent and empty and the windows of the school were without life. . .* First we feel ourselves alone on the playground, then we fix the playground squarely in Wales. After that, we can see the dark hills, the smoke, the cold winter and reddened knees. And after that—the longing, the desire to break free. *Up to now it had been remembered ground, but from here on it would be all exploration. He took a deep breath and went for the hills.*

And what is writing if not another way to head for the hills? Or another way to return, in order to break free again and again? The writer is simultaneously mapmaker and map, caught between two impulses. One is to be the ultimate tourist, not knowing your destination. The other is toward re-creation—accuracy of memory, a blueprint of all you know.

He began to imagine the long quietness of his gliding over the ice. He thought of thick ice, clear as glass, beneath which the cold fish swam, staring up with their goggle eyes at the sliding boys. He thought of ice like a dazzling mirror set in the hills, on which they could skim above their own images, each brilliant slider like two perfect boys—one upside down—joined at the feet.

Would we have found this place on our own? Or would we drive past, hardly aware of lives formed here, where schoolboys are *sliding through time with not a fall in mind, / their voices crying freely?* We'll never know. The proverbial chicken and egg. Looking out the window, I see what I expect to see. The text has seen to that. I enter the story. Entering the story, I find what I know I will find. I'm taken out into the world. One reinforces the other. So it's not revival that's at stake, although it may be for the writer. More an act of confirmation. A place where writer and reader can, for once, sit quietly at rest. We've crossed the border into shared territory.

"They're under the road too," said Denzil. "The same stones."
I looked down from the walls of Denzil's castle. It was easy to see the road, now that he'd said it. A discernible track, fainter green than the land around, marched straight and true, westward from the Roman circle, until it met the hedge. Even there it had defied nearly two thousand years of husbandry.

The land betrays its history. Layers and layers to be unearthed. Stories to be written, the accumulations of a lifetime. Maybe you have to leave in order to comprehend. Otherwise, what are you but another trace? Maybe the writer needs a longer view: *As we climbed we could see, a long way off, the ruins of an abbey, its solid wall so pierced by the procession of great arched windows through which we saw the lit hills behind that it appeared insubstantial, a tracery of stone. The long evening sun shone fully upon it, on the tall decay of its towers, on its useless pillars.*

That night, our waitress tells us she can't understand the Northern Welsh. "It's too deep," she says. I have visions of vowels, hard as stone, buried at the root of the tongue. Ted does not come. We linger over our coffee, hoping to see him again. Finally we walk out into darkness, past the small churchyard, down through the village streets where we can look in to see lives not our own. White cats in windows stare back at us. A late car pulls into a driveway and somewhere, deep in the house, a woman is pulling the meal from the oven, turning on lights, suddenly brisk and purposeful. Where does Ted come from, shuffling his way to the pub? We do not see him on this street, or the next. "You can set your watch by him." But tonight we must go to sleep without such assurance, and tomorrow we will leave. Yet he is a fixture: *Ordinarily a morose man, silent, possessed altogether by a refined melancholy, his single gesture toward speech would normally be a sigh of the slightest possible audibility, an exhalation as soft as the air on which it floated. He was a still, downcast man, hunched in his corner, effaced by sadness.*

Tomorrow we will leave. We will never know if Ted is alive or dead. And it will not matter. Not to us. Of course he's alive. He moves onto the page. Or steps *from* the page, and into the pub. We are not sure which.

But when tomorrow arrives, it brings its own surprises. Sometime in the night—a bracken-black night—someone has broken into our car. The lock on the passenger side has been skillfully forced and replaced; the plastic casing around the ignition has been hastily broken—shards are strewn everywhere. Oddly, it starts even without a key. And yet nothing is gone. We search the suitcases and bags we'd left inside, filled with gifts for people back home. Everything's intact. Even the single-malt whiskey is still there, wrapped in its distillery bag. They wanted nothing from us!

Who came down from the hills to this desolate spot, jimmied our doors, and left—probably frightened in the act? The local police have an answer. "Hippies." They prefer to be called "traveling people," those who live outside society, ranging across the

British Isles in a caravan of odd vehicles. They know their rights. They camp on the commons, open moorland there for all to use, none to own. "Hippies," he says, and he's probably right. But we are forced to realize that we are the traveling people, tourists with our newly acquired Celtic jewelry, our wool sweaters, our coasters, our maps.

This time, we take the road to Llandovery, then cut quickly to the main roads, the ones that lead to Cardiff and a replacement car. The sign to Merthyr Tydfil tells us how small the distances really are. But we're already heading out, already leaving behind the heritage that is, after all, not our own. We have choices to make: we'll stop at Caerleon to see the Roman ruins—huge amphitheater, baths, soldiers' barracks; we won't be able to stop at Tintern Abbey, fifteen miles away. We don't have time. The Welsh of *Aberaeron* and *Llandrindod Wells* gives way to the harsher English sounds of *Dartmouth* and *Dorchester* and *Poole*.

Yet I have memories I cannot account for. I move beyond the glittering fact of summer. Already I can imagine the moors in autumn, the bracken gone to rust. Not the bright reds of October in New England, but the later, faded colors of November. Already I can picture the fog in the valleys, the slight dusting of snow. I can hear the sharp syllable of a dog's name on the wind, *Bob* or *Belle* or *Nick*, as the herder calls him in. Memories of his memories.

> The weathers and scenes of childhood remain long in a man's mind, and I tried to remember them; but when I searched among the images of the past I found myself too far away. I have traveled away from those places for half a lifetime. Their summers are thin and cold, their voices inaudible. It was then that I realized there is no place mine without the asking for it, no place where I belong by clear right.

In the end, the writer is an alien in his own land. Like the hawk, he is *a still point in the moving sky*. He has stepped outside the flow of time in order to fix the moment. He can never quite return. So he offers up the infinite, exiled spaces of his heart.

The hills open onto a wide plain; the mind quickens; there is something at the rim of the horizon, a white road that, when you find it, with its solid walls and hedges, its clear delineations, seems to know where it's going. What can you do but open the book and begin?

Lists

For the umpteenth time, we cross the Continental Divide. Christina and I have taken her sister's old Renault on the trip of its lifetime—due west from Chicago into Iowa, then cutting through Kansas into Colorado, and now, heading north into Wyoming and the Grand Tetons. The road winds upward and we soon add seven mountain goats to our list:

3 deer (2 bucks, 1 doe)
antelope (too many to count)
4 prairie dogs
6 jackrabbits
1 elk (we think)
1 moose
7 mountain goats.

In Jackson, we see three nuns in long black skirts, white coifs. We add them to the list: 3 nuns (joke). We push on another half hour. Without foothills, the mountains are sudden and massive.

They gleam in the distance. Unfortunately, the campsite at Colter Bay is full so we decide on Yellowstone, turning once to see the peaks in sunset, ragged black against pale purple. It's dark when we start a fire for hot dogs and beans. And even darker when the bear appears right over our shoulders, looking more curious than dangerous. We scramble into the car and lock the doors. Our food! The bear's nose is at my window. Christina opens her door, rushes out to grab the pot from the fire, rushes back again. We can't stop laughing. We eat inside as the bear inspects, in turn, each garbage can. We're honestly too young to be afraid.

But that is memory, subject to the ravages of time. Did we, maybe, stop at Jackson Lake? Go to Yellowstone the following day? There's no record. Not even the list, though we both remember making the list. We didn't even take cameras.

The bear (we must remember to add him to the list) is part of our decision not to pitch our tent. The bear—and the temperature. Too cold for the end of August. Mornings, there's a skin of ice on the water pails. Two guys working at the gas station tell us they're about to return to the university, that we can stay in the women's dormitory since there's bound to be some room. Just ask the girls in 202. But 202 is empty when we get there and we have no idea who we're looking for. We crawl into our sleeping bags and squeeze under their beds.

It's late when we hear them come in, whispering about men and work as they slide into the covers above us. The springs sag and creak. In the morning we wake at first light, but the beds are empty. They've come and gone, never realizing we were there. They will go through life without knowing we spent this night under their beds. All day in the car we imagine scenes in which, twenty years from now, we meet someone who worked as a waitress in Yellowstone the summer of 1960, stayed in room 202. Then we tell her where we slept. She doesn't believe us, even when we describe the top of her dresser, the huge stuffed bear with the pink bow on her pillow.

And that is reconstructed imagination. It seems as though that is what we would do, knowing us as I do. Do I remember the actual conversation? Almost, but not quite.

The land turns flat and hard. Outside Dubois, Wyoming, population 279, we have two flat tires in quick succession. The two young men in the tow truck only charge us for ten of the seventeen miles. We spend two nights waiting for foreign tires from Cheyenne. In the local diner, we discover how to say the name of the town—Doo Boys. In Nebraska, we add buffalo (1 herd) but we don't count cattle.

When I say "us," I must be talking about the combination. Apart, we are separate entities, but together we are who we are when we are with each other.

Scotland—Edinburgh—swallows us whole. In our combined life, we share an apartment, cook meals for each other every third evening, become members of the Dramatic Society. She acts; I direct. We share the streets around the university, the small shops in Tollcross where we buy our food, the bus routes between the two. But in our separate lives, the city comes to life for each of us in other ways. She does not share my daily lunch with Andrew and Neil at the refectory, may or may not note the mid-afternoon light over the castle, turning it dark against the sky. There are streets I know, scenes I have by heart, that are not hers. What we share is our joint history—college life, five days in a ship on the ocean, and our newfound sense of being American. By Thanksgiving, we have perfected a new list:

How about a chocolate ice cream cone?
Yeah, and how about a double cheeseburger?
Yeah, and how about peanut butter and jelly?
Yeah, and how about ripe bananas?
Or corn on the cob?
Yeah, and how about brownies?
And milkshakes that are thicker than milk?
And catsup instead of vinegar on chips?
And why don't they call them French fries?

And why are they so soggy?

And right now I could even stand fish sticks.

This is what we will remember when we are together again. What we did together, how we were together. We call this knowing someone, but it's really knowing ourselves when we're with the other.

I have the photograph: graduation, May 1963. There is my brother George, and Andrew with Christina's mother. My mother and father are there too, but they must have taken the picture. Andrew and I have been married for a year and soon we will return to Edinburgh where he will finish his degree. But for now, the past and future converge; our families converge; our friendship feels like forever.

And yet we do not see each other, not when Christina marries Gordon, not when my two sons are born, not when she writes from San Francisco to tell me of the births of Ethan or James or, later, red-haired Maggie. Our letters cross the continent, growing fewer and farther between. I dream her life and it is perfect: husband, three children, elegant home above the Bay. And when they divorce, there is soon another husband, and trips to New England, Europe. Christina becomes a Jungian analyst—an occupation I cannot imagine—and it seems to me that our paths would not intersect even if they crossed. What would we say to each other?

We would say what we always said. Which is whatever we happened to be thinking. But I do not know that.

It's been twenty-six years since we've seen each other. And so it is with skepticism—even with fear—that I arrange to meet her for lunch in August of 1989. Stan and I are on our way from Palo Alto to Oregon and we only have three hours to spare. She's just returned from Iowa where she had her father's name put on a headstone. He was buried with his parents, but never had a marker. Her father. I remember a silent man, sitting in his car, drinking. Her grandmother. I knew only the woman we visited in Waterloo who insisted we join her bridge club and made concoctions of coke, tea, and lemonade. The woman whose husband had died in the library while she was shopping in the Piggly Wiggly. The grey-haired woman I met who had once been young Pauline Ross, newly married, with dreams of her own.

When Christina opens the door I'm amazed at how much she is the self I think I know. She's wearing jeans and a cotton sweater and her short hair gives her angular face a kind of edge. She calls me by my maiden name. We take up where we left off. This is life on fast forward. We gloss over all the intervening years to get to where we are now. Because that is where our stories become one story.

So there's not enough space over lunch to get it all in. And we have to be polite, to tell Jonathan and Stan what we're talking about, to retell the stories. All too soon we're back in our car, heading for the bridge before rush hour. Stan and I begin to log our list of license plates. We keep track of every state and province we see. Out here, we see rare ones like Utah and Manitoba. Even Alaska, though once we saw Alaska on a narrow dirt road just outside Franklin, North Carolina.

On the way through Idaho and western Montana, we cross the Continental Divide so many times we wonder how the rivers know which way to flow. The map reveals a jagged line where water hovers on the brink of indecision. It comes as a surprise that the Missouri begins here, so far from where its water eventually meets the sea. This is a large country. You could get lost in it.

Later, in Yellowstone, we drive through acre after scorched acre. It's only a year since the big fire, and the blackened trees turn it into alien landscape. The trunks are lifeless but underneath them ground cover has already taken hold. There are purple flowers and it is strangely beautiful.

Stan and I reverse the original route, from Yellowstone through the Tetons and down the pass through Dubois. It's not much larger, though McDonald's seems to have caught up with everywhere. Still, we notice that the phone directory lists the ranches under their brands:

∞ (Lazy 8)
® (Circle R)
¥ (Y bar T).

Neither prairie nor mountain, this land is high and arid. It feels like more than two days to Cheyenne.

Time is hammered thin. I retrace my steps to recover the past. But the past accompanies me. What is there is always there, and what is gone remains forgotten. This is a new experience, with someone else, and I am not who I was, but who I am with him.

When the earthquake hits San Francisco during the World Series, we are in a rented house, three miles up a mountain in western Massachusetts, just below the border with Vermont. On the TV, the reporter is standing on the corner of Broderick and something. Broderick is Christina's street! I call. They're all fine. Cupboard doors flew open, some dishes fell off the shelves. Nothing else. But they'd gone to the game, and it took them hours to get home to discover the absence of damage. They live with this uncertainty as a matter of course.

The next summer my sons move to Seattle in an old Ford Ranger, solidly packed with futons, speakers, guitars. Please call me each evening, I ask, so I can sleep at night. And go to the Grand Tetons, I tell them. They'll stay in your memory forever. But they don't. Instead, they stop in the Badlands where they leave the truck to walk out into miles of windhewn rock. Whichever way they turn, it looks the same. They are old enough to be scared.

You cannot inherit memory. My sons will never see the mountains in my mind. But if they'd go there, they might find our memories intersect. They could carry some small piece of me, of the world as I might have seen it.

The airline map of flight paths creates a spider web. And so we begin to spin the subtle filament that connects us to Seattle. We visit in January when the days are short and you are glad to step inside the Starbucks on the corner for a cup of hot coffee. You are glad when the clouds part briefly and you glimpse the

Cascades or have a hint of summer in the ephemeral glare of water. Then the plane to San Francisco hugs the coast and you hardly notice the sun; suddenly you are watching the shadow of the plane ascend until there's a perfect match, a jolt, and you have landed.

George is waiting at the gate. Noon—and nowhere to go until tomorrow when we will visit my Uncle Willy in his nursing home down the peninsula. We drive the rented car up and down the hills, charming in the shock of sunlight. Broderick. There it is, turn the corner, let's see if she's at home. And so we mount the steps laughing, impromptu.

Jonathan hardly seems surprised. Then he realizes what we don't know. In the dark living room, he tells us the news. Christina is upstairs, resting in her battle against breast cancer. Sixty percent of her lymph nodes involved. How can I not have known? But it's only been six months since she first felt the lump. Jonathan disappears, then reappears. She wants me to come up, he says. She's lying on the bed and as she rises I am struck with the physical changes, the bald head, the emaciated body. Then we hug and nothing has changed. We start where we left off, where we never stopped.

The most amazing thing is the way she speaks matter-of-factly about her possible death. It's real to her. And its reality means that she can see the world in terms of it. Death does not circle just out of reach; she places it on the bed before us where we each speak the word—and go on.

So memory, now, is reduced to the physical body. It does not outlive us. What does she make of the small piece of her life that is contiguous with mine? How does that fit into the larger and larger circles, the widening ripples that, when it is over, we call a life?

Christina jokes that her family likes her better now that she forgets things. She has to make lists, like the rest of them. Little things, like dry cleaning and bread for breakfast. But she is waiting for the day when she is not so fuzzy-headed and can hold details intact, can fit the pieces together to make a whole. She plans to live a while longer, she says, and she'd like to understand her own story.

We decide to go downstairs for wine and cheese. Christina glances at the wig and laughs. She doesn't wear it. She always put it on backwards, couldn't make it work. Besides, she hasn't seen George for twenty-eight years, he won't remember her *with* hair. Later, we decide on a restaurant. Jonathan hasn't been out for months, it will be good for him. She refuses to wear a wig because, she says, she wants people to be aware of how *real* this is, how many women are going through a similar battle. We hide it—even from ourselves. She refuses to pretend what is happening doesn't happen. It happens, in the prime of life, when your first son is about to get married, when your daughter has two years of high school to finish, when your new husband is still so new it wants to feel like forever. It happens, and if you speak about it, you will give it dignity. It calls your whole life into question and, if you are Christina, you examine the question and discover some answers of your own. You own your life, completely.

All lists are incomplete. But memory goes on, renewing itself. This day will become whatever it will be. It will live in those of us who shared it, sometimes large, sometimes so small it slips through the fingers and is gone. I do not know what it will mean to anyone else. To her. For me, it will be the day she gave me the gift of her honesty.

On the way home, she is visibly tired. Still, we find time to tell Maggie, who seems hungry for her mother's past, about the trip across the mountains and the bear and how it's only now that we realize we should have been afraid. We tell the story of sleeping under the beds of unknown waitresses and, yes, we'd still like to meet the fifty-year-old women who think they only dreamed the sound of someone breathing, the muted rustle of fabric as bodies turn in sleep.

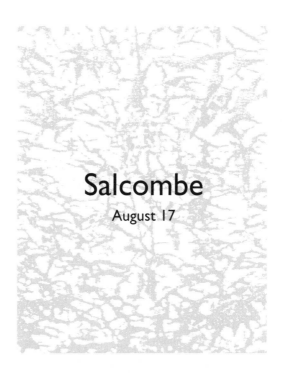

Salcombe

August 17

At last, open sea. We crest a hill and there it is—wider than the fields, less fluent. Blue and forever. On another day, it would be wild and grey. It would break over the sandbar, flinging itself toward shore.

Today the sun shines for the annual regatta. Overlooking the estuary, we watch as myriad white sails stitch the water in a crazy quilt. I could look up on the cliff, searching for Noel's old summer house. I could look to the opposite shore—there—where William and Matthew took the ferry, found driftwood and shells. I lean against the railing while twenty years pass. I am here. What I want most is to walk down into town with you. And later, as the afternoon drifts by, I want to drive the coast road toward Dartmouth, stopping at Torcross for scones with clotted cream. I want to sit outside in plastic chairs carefully placed at the edge of the seawall and I want to meet an elderly couple who will tell us how they remember the American troops practicing for the landing at Normandy. I want to drive home to the inn with its thick thatched roof. Tomorrow, I want to go where tiny ponies range for miles over heathland and granite outcroppings. I want to climb out on High Tor where the rocks spill from the earth like jagged lava. *Scissors cut paper / paper covers stone / stone breaks scissors.* Our childhood game must have come from Devon where rock pierces sky, sky covers water, water erodes rock.

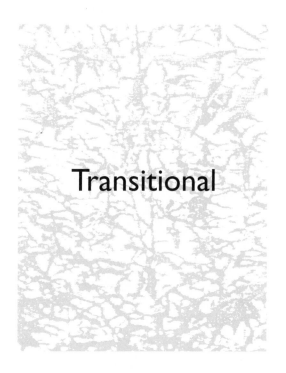

Transitional

Stop, now move a little to the left, no, just a bit higher, okay, good, now smile! Click. We're frozen, forever happy on a day taken out of our lives. The photographer thinks nothing of intruding. He wants to catch you as you never were, there, on those rocks—not here, where you were sitting in warm sun, listening to the incessant beat of the ocean, lost in reverie. No, he wants you there, in the best light, with the sky at your back. He wants you to find the photo, years from now, and recognize yourself. Or else he wants to find it himself, thinking *how like her* . . . But that is not me. I was not there. Nothing in me would stand woodenly smiling on that rock. I would be lower, crouching by the tidepool, watching anemones open and close their underwater garden.

Framed. Caught in the unnatural pose that plays to story—to version—but never to memory itself. Frozen, as though life were not that fluid field of time we move through. As though, outside the camera's lens, there were no others to call to, no ocean that opens to endless seascape, then drums again on the shores of Ireland. As though the mind did not wander wherever it wanted. As though the smile were real.

That's why the album lies. I smile back at myself as if all moments were alike. But memory is often angry or sad or, at the very least, pensive. I do not recognize the happy child. Here's one: I'm on the top of the woodpile, wearing red and white striped overalls. And another: I'm holding a rabbit. My face is buried in its back. What I see is hair and fur and a deep undisturbed contentment that calls it all back. I miss that rabbit. I miss that child.

But the photos are monochromatic, so memory itself supplies the red stripes. Memory makes my hair catch the sun and my fingers dig deep in soft fur. Two kinds of memory, sewn back to back, like a reversible scarf so each time you put it on, you carry both. On one side, memory that is static, locked in past tense—vivid, yes, but relegated to the art of anecdote: the stuff of narration, given the frame of beginning, middle, and end. On the other side, memory that relives itself, always in the present tense, ever ready and available as it floods over you with all the emotions intact; it's there, swimming the shallows, ready to surface in an instant—but an instant you cannot predict. These memories make themselves part of the day so that, standing here, I am also there, fused to a past that has yet to run clear.

On the car stereo, samba from Brazil. *Ela não gosta de mim.* The words, over and over, a refrain that means, literally, *she doesn't like me.* Or, even more literally, *she has no liking for me.* Or would *affection for* be better? Or *taste?* In English, it's ludicrous, but in Portuguese *like* slides so easily into *love* that it makes its own sense. *She loves me not*—over and over—the daisy petals fall, and I am filled with longing.

I struck a blow / to the cat / but the cat / didn't die. / Dona Chica / loves herself / and the cry / the cat makes / is meow. Who could think up a song like that? But it winds through the streets of Rio and brings back color and texture. The tiles of the kitchen floor are small and white and they shine even in the shade of the awning.

They are cool on bare feet and, if you want, you can step through the open doorway onto the balcony where you can look down on children playing soccer, or across to where palm trees open their fans to the sky. You can stand there and listen to the soft thud of jackfruit falling in the garden next door, or you can imagine your-self one floor below in the apartment of your landlord—Pericles— with his dark leather footstools and his salty liquor. Alive. The cat makes a sound.

How much do we need the connective tissue of transition? We stitch the singular moments of our lives to each other simply because *they happened to us.* That's all we need for internal conti-nuity. But language makes fools of us. How can we convey what we want others to know and feel? What we have felt? All the flotsam that surrounds the feeling?

J'ai peur. How weak compared to *I'm afraid.* The French "have" so many things—fear, hunger, malaise. In English, we embody what we feel. We *are* hungry—are hunger itself. Immediate. I suppose the French have fear until it fills them and becomes less a noun and more a state of being. I suppose the words do not come to them in awkward translation.

Ela não gosta de mim. Words bridge the gap. The phrase winds itself around my fingers and tugs the strings of memory. But it was another life I was living—detached and ethereal. The sun was too hot; children died of it. Or they were crushed by faulty elevators, or trapped on the roofs of burning buildings, or their skulls were cracked on the sides of hotel swimming pools. Fear was everywhere. It trailed me up and down the narrow streets. I could hear its footsteps.

Here's a frame: a wedding on the lawn. As I tell it now, with hindsight, it's clearly one-of-a-kind. The stuff of anecdote. My Aunt Margaret had a surprise wedding. She invited her friends to a party and then the minister arrived and she got married. The guests were handed a ready-made story. *Remember when Margaret Randels got married?* Or: *I bet I can top that one—I once went to a surprise wedding.*

But I was seven. I was wearing new shoes and a new green dress and my braids were tied with yellow ribbons. I was seven, and I fell from the swing. My new black patent-leather shoes slipped on the seat and I flew, for an instant, before I landed in the dust.

This summer we have returned to the house we rented last year. It sits on the top of a hill in the Berkshires, ten miles from the Vermont border. We've returned to an alternate life—one with long hours watching mist rise from the mountains, long hours alone with the clean sweep of blank page. Last year, it was autumn and the hillsides were bronze and woodsmoke stained the air with its kippered taste. Each house tucked itself into an envelope of hills. Now, it is summer and everything is the shade of watercolor—cool green, like ragged fern. The houses hide as we drive through the dusty back roads. Still, we find them: farmhouses with wide porches and crumbling barns; white capes with the sprawling rooflines of each new century's addition; brown-shingled cottages perched over streams. In each, we live a new life. We place ourselves inside their rooms, sit at their painted red tables or walk their wide pine floors, look through wavery glass to test the view we would have—if we were other.

This, I have come to understand, is a form of editing. I come into this rented house and make it mine. Instantly, rugs must be moved. The red one is better here, with all the windows. The white one should go in the darker room. If I shift this lamp it will catch that reflection. Put the apples in the wooden bowl; the glazed one (with its dark purple) is fruit enough by itself. Now the blue chair—there—in the corner. How right it suddenly is.

But how do I know it is right? *They* obviously like it the way it was. With rugs and chairs it hardly matters, but literature is another story. It occurs to me that if we can train ourselves to read as editors, we might do the same with memory. Pick and choose—shape the life. *Yes, thank you, I'd like that one for this circumstance.* If that were possible, however, we'd also know what to do with history—those famous mistakes we should never repeat. If so, I'd know now, as Saddam Hussein masses his troops in Kuwait, which war to turn to. And, in the end, what *was* the lesson of Vietnam? What we seem to have learned is not why I demonstrated in the streets, not why McCarthy's blue-and-white daisy faded year by year on the back of my red VW. Should we turn to Hitler and World War II? And how much of World War II was caused by World War I? And before that, what? In the end, of course, each moment in history is discrete—and the lessons are ephemeral at best.

And if I could find answers, my country hardly wants to know my conclusions. Tomorrow American soldiers will fly into Saudi Arabia and I will place my chair where, if you are careful in the early morning, your eye will catch the glint of dew on the web, there, between those branches, see, it stretches itself in sunlight and disappears on the breeze. It's summer, and nature too is an editor. August, but some days there's a chill in the air and, by the fence, one tree is tipped with orange. Tomorrow will be hot and humid, stepping back into July, reluctant to give itself over. And I must look at these hills with summer eyes, peering deep into the forest or behind the hedgerow in order to glimpse those other lives we think we want to be living.

August. One yellow leaf pasted to the rainswept window, the color of nostalgia. The early maple tinged. One step back from green. One step back. Step on a crack, you'll break your mother's back.

I am seven. I am wearing new shoes and a new green dress and my braids are tied with yellow ribbons. I am seven, and I fall from the swing. My new black patent-leather shoes slip on the seat and I fly, for an instant, before I land in the dust.

I fly out into loss. It hits me and I double over to catch my breath. My throat tightens. I am about to lose something I love. I fly, and then whatever wings I have will not comply. I fall into the narrowness of the day. Over and over, like a song's refrain, loss beyond my control. Over and over, because there is no frame. I cannot put it to rest.

Everything outside my window is changing, and yet the view remains constant. It's a matter of preference—long or short range. I choose the microscope: berries move from green to yellow to red; the birch tree bends in the wind one evening and next morning its leaves are silver and charged. That's why I bring the outside in. Pick the tiger lilies and arrange them in the vase, find the place where they will focus the eye on their spot of eccentric color. I suppose I'm making a still-life. A kind of translation.

What has been said recedes to that other world—the realm of words forgotten. A past tense of the past tense. The ghost of used words binds us. And so I have her always with me—a seven-year-old girl, wearing a green dress. I pull her into this life and she wants to speak. She knows the swing—and its treachery. She knows what lies on the other side of flight.

The local video store has a sign in its window: WE CAN PUT YOUR MEMORIES ON VIDEOTAPE. But memory isn't memory until it is past tense. It is subjective, filled with internal voice. They might capture the event—but not the memory. To do that, I would have to hold the camera, select the angle of vision. And to hold the camera is to efface the self. To become an impersonal eye. A cold and singular lens.

Remember the fight you had with your brother? I ask the fifth graders. *Remember how right you were?* Titters. *Well, forty years from now you will still be right. Only trouble is, in his memory he will be right.* Laughter. They know it is true. Two sides to every fight. Two versions of every story. We know that neither of us was wholly right, but does knowledge stop the flow of feeling, the intensity with which we remember our indignation? *Have some perspective,* my mother would say—meaning learn to see the other side. But I *had* a perspective—have it still—and it comes with the force of conviction. It comes complete, dressed and ready, with only one pair of eyes, and they are as green as my own.

It is not just poetry that is lost in translation; it is the cultural history, the family history, the whole long chain of being that culminates in a word. From one language to another, one family, one person to another, there is a dead space—a vacuum into which the word is plunged before it blooms on the other side, charged with a meaning and a context that almost fits, like a borrowed coat.

If we arrange our lives in the album, something is missing. It is not sequence that keeps us intact. It's that fluid self, moving by osmosis, from past to present to past. It's what isn't in the photograph—the blurred edges, the blank spaces, the figure outside the frame. We do not live *in* the present; we *are* a present moment that is cumulative. The infernal *now* is simply that—colorless space into which we bring our calendars, suspenders, shampoo. We fill it with our clutter. And our clocks.

Shampoo. Odd, my hair acts one way in Massachusetts and another in New York. It's the water. It determines which shampoo sits on the shelf. The ads can say whatever they like—can show you woman after woman with flounce and flair—but it's trial and error and the make-up of the water that tells you which shampoo to buy.

Don't compare apples and oranges. How many times have I heard it? But why ever not? At least they have something in common, some reason to make the distinctions the good critic makes. Among fruits, you may know which you prefer, which is more practical for the picnic, which will add substance to the sauce, or make the better pie. I'd say don't compare telescopes to Queen Anne's lace, though then the mind rushes to see the connections. Lawn mowers to chocolate? Sidewalks to cigars? *Ain't got no apples in Florida*, the migrant boy writes for me, and I know he knows the difference between apples and oranges, this life and that.

Conjunctions are the key to transition. The connective thread of narrative. *Then* and *then* and *thus* and *yet*—all building up to the *therefore* or the *furthermore*. The hinges that fold the story on itself and then help it unfold again, following its tenuous trail of connections. Maybe that's why life in another country is mysterious—things seem to happen without cause, often without effect. The ear goes into high gear, desperately trying to fit a sound to a meaning. The eye registers everything, in hopes that sight and sound will eventually converge. So Rio is buried deep inside a swirl of color and sound, nebulous and inexact. *What was it like?* people ask, and my answers are vague. How to explain the offerings to *Exú*—wine bottles and cigarettes discovered on the curb each morning? Or the ache in my throat as I stand at the window listening to the lazy chatter of maids in the courtyard? Or the taste of *farofa*, like buttery sawdust?

How can I show you the men and women pulling on their nets in Bahia? They work at a feverish pitch, tugging two ropes, tightening their long net into a circular trap, working against the swell of the sea and gusts of wind from an oncoming storm. They work as they have always worked, singing, digging bare heels in harsh sand. They work knowing that *Imenja*, the goddess of the sea, covets them, would quickly snatch them away to her underwater lair. I can say what they do, but I cannot put their ropes in your hands. You might feel the tug, but you do not have hundreds of years at your back or the song on your lips.

I know that, in Portuguese, it is possible to feel the presence of the *orixás*. The gods inhabit the language. They live in drumbeats, in heartbeats, in the beat of feet on the floor. Their songs are full of throaty darkness, like a woman making love. And I know that in Portuguese it is not possible to think certain thoughts because there are no precise words for them. You can't say, *put it on the coffee table.* You have to say—and think—*put it on the little table over there near the couch.* A precision of abstraction.

How the Germans must wait in expectation, holding all possibility in their ears, until the verb chinks into place, sending a shock wave back through the sentence. How language must shimmer as they wait, and then how quickly it settles into meaning, forever cut off from the very imagination it unlocked. And why is the wasp at my window so persistent? He hovers there with his shiny black body suspended, his legs disproportionately long, looking as though he should land, but instead he hovers at the glass, waiting for a verb. He is a German sentence.

It is said that the Koran was written down on scraps of leather, palm leaves, bits of camel bone. Muhammad's rhythmic prose,

140

told to him, he claimed, by God, was gathered and arranged into chapters. Some ancient editor felt the need to give his wisdom form—to move from the spoken to the written word, with all its complications.

Maybe peace is a kind of transition. A hiatus between wars. Certainly we mark history with war—we date events and place them in a context. Nothing was ever called the "hundred years' peace." War, and the memory of war. Because, in the end, memory is all we have. When I was three, I was afraid of our neighbor, Johnny Harr. I was afraid of the strange, contorted sounds he made, his throat destroyed by mustard gas. There is no video, and yet he struggles in slow motion, his raspy voice and twisted face becoming what my mother tells me is a smile.

Yesterday we drove through old logging roads in the forest. We could have become lost, circling till nightfall. Each intersection looked alike. Each curve identical. Then suddenly, in the middle of nowhere, an abandoned cemetery. People had lived nearby—and died. All we have left is the record of their deaths. And stone walls that wind their way through the woods—no sign of a house or barn, just the relics of field, filled with second-growth forest. And maybe, if we were here in the springtime, a lilac blooming out of place in the maples and pines. People lived and died—Taylors and Goulds and Hunts—and nothing is left but the name of a road on a map and a tiny clearing. Who wouldn't want to be buried here, forgotten, swallowed by sunlight splaying through leaves and the occasional call of a bird? In winter snow must fill this spot, drifting and swirling around the grey stones, maybe so deep that even the graveyard becomes only field, and field extends to sky, and nothing is what it was, or what it will become.

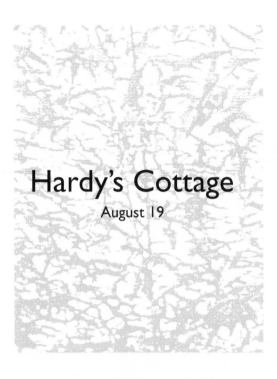

Hardy's Cottage
August 19

The morning news brings reports of Gorbachev under house arrest at his summer dacha, tanks in Moscow. Stan and I go down to breakfast agitated and apprehensive. The British vacationers, with their ubiquitous reserve, seem to go about their business unaffected. Eggs with bacon, grilled tomato, marmalade for the toast. And not a word about international affairs. Perhaps it's the legacy of the fifties—communist threat, heads ducked under desks, Alger Hiss as evil incarnate—but it seems to us that the present Russian coup should warrant some breakfast conversation. Everyone speaks in lowered tones, polite, inconsequential.

Still worried, we tune the car radio to news programs and find our way through Stinsford where Hardy's heart is buried in the churchyard, then, via a series of almost unreadable signs, to Higher Bockhampton and Hardy's birthplace. You can't drive all the way because a gate blocks the last mile of narrow road. Parking in the lot, we see a sign that points to an alternative path.

142

And so we come to it from behind, up from the edge of the heath, through Thorncombe Wood, discovering—too late—the walking sticks for sale at what should be the beginning of the trek back to the car.

It's tiny and, to American eyes, charming. The garden is delightful—a maze of flower beds connected by grassy paths, green beyond green. Roses climb the cottage walls. Inside, it takes no time at all to walk through the two rooms downstairs, the three small bedrooms, to look out the window where Hardy is said to have written page after page leaning on the sill. If inspiration seized him outdoors, he wrote on leaves, wood chips, pieces of stone or slate. This is where dreams were shaped, where an impoverished mother would give her son the *Aeneid* when he was four years old. Here, where life was rough-and-tumble, the young Hardy imagined himself at the writing table now housed in the town museum, imagined himself as London's darling. And yet he returned here, peopling the pages with tradesmen and chamber maids, country folk who knew the ways of the nearby villages—this territory he thinly disguised as Wessex, extending its boundaries to include Dartmoor with its wild ponies, its red earth.

In the cramped living room, a man is talking to the guide. He's read all the books but *Jude the Obscure*. Ironically, he's a bricklayer, working on the restoration of a cathedral in Kent.

The way back is shorter, flatter, past a row of cottages, a pony in a field. Nettles sting my bare legs and I'm glad when the lane widens and the spires of Dorchester can be seen in the distance. Nearly a hundred and fifty years ago, Hardy walked the miles there to school. I am only an American tourist, come to pay homage, come to understand what cannot be understood—the dream that drives a man beyond his natural boundaries. And so my eyes lift to a plane crossing this landscape now, connecting it to a world larger than all of England. I worry about a man with a map on his head, a man who once stepped from his car and shook the hands of ordinary people.

143

I do not yet know that Yeltsin will stand on the balcony of the Russian White House and offer a glimpse of the future. I do not know that three days from now, as I step off the plane in Toronto, the coup will be over and the people will have prevailed. I only know that the sky has been altered by man's dream of flight. I can never see what Tess saw alone under stars.

Songs to Undo the Spring

And do not call it fixity,
Where past and future are gathered. Neither movement from nor towards,
neither ascent nor decline. Except for the point, the still point,
There would be no dance, and there is only the dance.
—T. S. Eliot, "Burnt Norton"

I. WATCHING

George and I are lying. Our mother has come back from shopping and we tell her, with deep conviction, that we have each practiced half an hour on the piano. We need to do this in order to have time to do the things we think we need to do. Otherwise, we are in a cage called *Sonatina*. We lie only when it is necessary: just exactly where we were when we were where we were not supposed to be, that sort of lie. We hardly think of them as lies since they save us from the greater lie.

How can she believe us? She's been gone for an hour and now she is asked to imagine the house filled with perfect Bach, notes filling the room without hesitation. She is asked to find herself dancing to a tune we cannot play. She can't be that gullible, but she plays along. This is the dance, then—this song and dance, give and take, in and out of mother and child. No one believes us, but we begin to believe ourselves. At our next lesson, we insist how much we have practiced, how hard the piece is. The pencil reaches out and raps my knuckles. Miss Curtis does not allow the hands to sink below the keyboard.

Curl the fingers. Make an arc above the keys. Let the music enter the instrument from the fingertips. Black and white. Each note falls on a deaf ear. I push down the mute pedal, play on and on in muffled silence; morning comes through the window, streaking the rug. The music blends with the day—grey, lifeless to the ear.

The eye is alive. The iris narrows. Black and white, the photograph waits for me to fill it in. The house is yellow with white pillars, green shutters, geraniums in the flower pots beside the steps. Aunt Margaret rides a bright red tricycle across the porch, knees to her chin. We laugh and the shutter snaps. Aperture. F-stop. Knees to her chin, she will not die. She will ride off, legs circling, laughing. The eye is alive. It sees again what it has seen. Sees itself seeing. Time folds back on itself like a sea of cloth, making waves that break over our heads. We drown in its infinite crashing.

How sad to see spring leave so quickly. The tulips are gone and I never even filled a vase to put them on the table. Never brought the outside in. What's left is what's to come. The lilac is still a purple haze, tightly closed fists and a pungent odor that catches you off guard when you've gone past. The peonies are promise—hard, round balls, tiny galls perched stiffly at the tip of the stem. They will swell, burst around a fissure of white, waiting for the ants who will strip the cover and let them flare. In a day they will flourish, nodding their heads along the hedge. And then, all too soon, the petals will droop and curl, remnants on the pavement.

The eye records. The shutter snaps. Holds still the childhood at the top of the stairs. The way dusk filtered through the screens. The haze of wavy lines above the street. Holds, still, the sight of music as dancers move below. The shoes say it all. One, two, and then shift. Back, two, and then glide. Toe in, then around. The sight of sound—a blur that shimmers like patterns on silk.

The eye recalls. How bright. In Rio, sun bleaches the buildings and each house shines white, capped with its roof of orange tiles. The palm trees splay their leaves and light trickles through fingers of green. In the distance the *favelas* spread a chaos of color on the hillsides. A flurry of song. The sound of a rooster rising into sunlit air. From a distance, there is no smell of stagnant water. No chalky dust on the beds. From a distance, no one is alone. No one grieves.

Come down from the hillside to where the people work. Ride with them each morning as they stream from bus to bus, hours of swaying in the heat before they can begin to cook and clean, rinse and sweep, reel in the awnings and set the table, bring out the strong coffee and bread. Follow them into the tiled courtyards where their brooms catch fallen petals—the unfettered pickings of the night. A night so deep and purple that even grief can sleep.

Watch the signer for the deaf. The fingers move so rapidly. The hands make pictures in the air. Sound caught in gesture. Gesture held in memory. The eye an ear that listens. The hands a mouth that responds. Language locked in silence. This must be the language of dance—every feeling given its moving form.

Dance with me here, in this year of memory, as though time itself were blue and iridescent. Dance me back to twenty, his arm at my shoulder, the moon a wing at my back. The sound of traffic whirring like cicadas. The occasional screech or honk that punctuates the night. Nothing but city sounds, and cars in two steady streams—one white, one red, one rolling forward as the other recedes. And if I met him today would I walk right on by? How would we recognize the past?

May. May. *Mother, may I?* A stone in the fist. Guess which one. See. The eye can fool you. See. I make a movement, feint, pretend. You choose the left, but it's in the right. Right where it always was. Right where I forced your eye away. Stone in the heart. Hard. Hardened. See. The heart can fool itself. What it wants is never what it gets. I thought you loved me. No, *he* loved me, and he is gone. Let me show you the photograph. There we are. You are looking at me across a table. Eyes leave a print; memory is film. Open the aperture—there is room for an image of love.

Open the aperture. The film will record only what is there: those birds on the telephone wires—a line of black shapes against the white sky. And if one shakes itself loose, rises out of the camera's range, who would know enough to miss it? I have walked on Ilkley Moor and heard larks out of the range of sight. The sky opens and they dive into view. They were there all along—peripheral sound.

And if love won't come? Well, there's time, and the swirl of seasons. June will be too hot, and heavy. I want to lie down in tender grass. I want to pick violets and put them in a jelly jar. I want my mother back, with her false delight. I want to hear her say *how lovely* and take the wilted offering. I pretend that if she came I would not lie. I hold out my hands. They are my mother's hands—filled with foreign money. *Take what you need*, she says, unable to count, to keep track of cruzeiros. Take what you need, and the hands disappear. They are your hands, and you will not dance. They are your eyes, and you will not look at me across the table. They are your words, and they hurt and hurt.

But May will not grieve, even if I want it to. It shimmies forth, the color of forget-me-nots. The strap of its gown falls over its shoulder. Effervescent. Green. *Your Christmas is showing!* My friend's mother's voice in my ears. She died last year. Her name was Jewel. My friend says she has finally stopped grieving, but on Sunday afternoons when the phone rings, she sometimes expects to hear her voice. My friend has learned to take long walks on the mountain. To give herself a present as well as a past.

May is all present-tense. Pert. Particular. Leaves flicker at the upstairs windows and sometimes the evening light is seductive. I would ride its back into summer. But this is the long song of springtime. The moon shivers on the canal. A sign. Something ended, something begun. Borrowed and blue. Torn from the hem of time. What's this in our bed like a seam? Something between us. Something that grows. A weed. Or a wall.

I watch myself watching. I take notes on my own disappointment. My mother reaches out her hand. Money scatters like confetti. The empty swing flies out—dark against the sky. On the ground, I cry and cry. No one can comfort me; I will let no one comfort me. I cherish my grief. Black and white, shiny, it glitters.

The crocus has come and gone. Green pushes out of the ground and the mind is filled with the promise of yellow and red. Such a long wait, restless, remembering green, remembering sunlight through venetian blinds making a ladder on the rug. Remembering, through each grey day, the music of summer and weddings on the lawn. My braids flying back, my knees pumping the swing, the sky so bright that the sun breaks into splinters that fracture the eye.

2. LISTENING

George and I are crouching at the bottom of the stairs. One of us will have to make the mad dash up to flip the light switch on the landing. Usually I am elected. I bite my lip, get set, then sprint as hard as I can up the steps. If I get there in time, if I don't stumble or fumble, I will once again avoid an encounter with the green-eyed monster. Meanwhile, George keeps watch so he can scream for help if something happens.

We believe in the green-eyed monster. He lives up there in the darkness and he wants to get us. We know this because Hank Hagey told us so. *Careful,* he said to us one night, *the green-eyed monster will get you.* And it grew suddenly real—horrid and vindictive, living at the top of our stairs.

Hank Hagey tells stories so that you see them. When freight trains stream past on the tracks near our house, we know that Stephen Brewster is at work. Stephen is a large chicken—so large she uses boxcars as her roller skates. Sometimes her colors fade, and then people have to put up ladders and scaffolding to paint her mammoth comb. She eats a ton of hamburgers at one sitting. We love the stories of Stephen—even the cleverness of her name which, we are shown, is Step Hen, Be Rooster.

Hank Hagey lives in the two-room apartment in our house, and he has become nearly a part of the family. George and I are almost always welcome and he almost always has some sort of tale. His laughter fills the room. We love it. We love the huge hen and all her shenanigans. But we are afraid of the green-eyed monster that, according to Hank, is waiting expressly for us. And in the dark we hear, among the other sounds, its steady breathing, its jealous prowling near our beds.

It is there, now, waiting in the horrifying familiarity of dream. It is there, at the top of the stairs, long after George has grown up and gone, leaving me with no one to call for help, no one to save me from my desires. And you are there, troubling my sleep, removed to third person singular, as though you did not share my bed but walked through it, receding in the distance, the unidentifiable *he* of my internal stories.

Listen. Country music on the radio. The open window trails it through the streets. Reba McEntire hits her high note and the voice quivers—it does not falter, or fade, but rather dips in its own sweet dance, catches each throat-tightening moment of your past and holds it out on a platter of sound. You could be younger. You could dance. You could bend backwards over his arm and let time stop, briefly, before you straighten, go on with your life. You could forget how you would not dance, self-conscious, observing yourself as though you were observed.

Under the cover of darkness, you could forget your body. You could erase the self. Neither from nor towards, but something embedded long before you learned the infernal "I" of your first sentence. Your fingers read the braille of someone else's skin. The body on the bed does not belong to you. It has grace. Clarity. It moves with the current, swirling, then churning, hovering over itself, awed at its effortless dancing. It balances at the edge of sound, then, suddenly, slides over the rim—to lie pooled, drifting counter-clockwise, a trace of froth, like spent fury. It is its own season.

April has its patterns, its crazy quilt of weather. Grey sky, rain and more rain, a smattering of snow, and now, today, sixty degrees and sun. There is a crocus in the yard, pushing up from beneath the residue of leaves. I rush to buy a rake and uncover it. Now the whole yard is in need. If I don't hurry, what will happen to the daffodils, the tulips?

They come up. Recycled. Always and ever. Here, and in my backyard at home. Though home is only a photograph, black and white, held in memory so that Kathy Sanford does not die and the streets stay slow and shimmery and our bicycles move down them in slow-motion, wobbling on their fat tires, our legs pumping and pumping into the future.

There are others. The one where I ride the merry-go-round in my bright red skirt. I am lifted easily up, reaching for the brass ring. Maybe you see me, in your mind's eye, neither rising nor falling, but held on the cusp, my arm outstretched, my skirt shifting in the breeze while the horse casts its wild eye backwards.

I live with someone who calls a hyacinth an iris. Why does that matter? And how did I learn to identify flowers as they emerge from sleep? This is my past—a litany of color that swirls in its own galaxy. Days rise out of the mist: my father transplanting the flowering quince; dandelions buttoning the lawn; my perch in the apricot tree, where white blossoms drop, like snow, in the breeze. Images fixed on the retina—a disease of the inner eye. In them, I fall off the swing on the day of my Aunt Margaret's wedding. My new shoes slip on the polished seat and I fly, briefly, as though my heart, too, were lifted above the ordinary lawn. How many times can you fly in a lifetime? How many times can the heart detach itself?

Count them. Each one has a story to tell, a name attached. Each one has a moment when the body danced, the eye forgot to see. Or forgot to look, so the sidelong glance is all that is remembered. At the center, something grows sharp like a knife in the ribs. And inside that, the music spirals back to its own beginnings in the inner ear. And inside that, the silence that precedes thought. Knows only its profound depth. Knows everything it is not.

Deep in the pupil, a mirror. The world floats past. Seen by the one who looks into the other's eye. Secondhand. Distanced. Deep in the pupil, what is seen is what is heard. Deepest blue, with a dusting of pink. Inside the shell, the sound of the sea. Inside the sea, the shape of the shell.

The beaches of Rio are scalloped, a hemline of white bordered with blue. In the air, kites dip then go taut, a thousand artificial birds above the sand. *Kibon, kibon,* the call of the vendors rises above the hum of human conversation. The popsicles are nested in ice—lemon, guava, coconut. The taste of the tropics—musty, muted, slightly worse for wear. *Kibon, kibon,* the waves make a rhythm that beats, like a drum, even into sleep. The sun is the enemy. The umbrellas drop their shade in circles on the sand.

And if grief is the vulture that circles the city, riding the thermals, then it is a quick, black grief that swoops suddenly and will not let go. It is the grief of time gone wrong and a life out of kilter. It is arsenic in the bloodstream and amoeba in the bowel. It kills slowly, eating away at every good thought you ever had. It dries up under the withering fire of epithet. You are the man on the beach calling, calling. He seems to want something, but he is so far away. He has candles to light in case of death. And death is ever-present, here, in the land of so much light.

What do I hear in the land of dream? *Kibon, kibon.* Death makes its jealous claim. There used to be another in the bed, but he is long gone. I reach out and touch the coldness he has turned to me. His sound is blue—like an angry sea, like shadow on snow.

My heart rushes up the stairs. At the top, the switch. If I am quick, I will save myself once more. George calls out to me—I see his open mouth, but his words are lost. Let us assume that as words enter the ear, they grow loud for a time, then fade and disperse. This is the way things die, by degrees of letting go. And yet this spring's magnolia is proof of something else. Each petal falls, mapping a circular plane, reaching for some exact center.

3. DANCING

George and I are lying at the top of the stairs, peering over the edge between the bannister rails, holding our breath so we will be almost invisible. The doorbell rings. We hear footsteps and then our mother's turquoise skirt comes into view. The door opens—a flurry of voices and stamping of boots and then, briefly, a lick of cold air drifting upward. We see shoes, skirts, belts, but no faces. There is no way to see the faces without being seen. So we listen, trying to guess which guests have arrived. The new-comers drift into the living room with the others and we try to pick individual voices from among the swirl of sound, the amaz-ing world that has parties from nine to midnight, filled with laugh-ter and the clink of ice in glasses and the occasional punctuation of political discussion. A world of 78s and phonographs and music floating upward step by step.

My parents' parties are innocent. Costume balls. Bridge games. Sing-alongs. Cocktail parties that end, sometimes, with a late-night meal. Once a wedding in the side yard, the whole day bright with expectation. And then my Uncle Ray was really my uncle, because he married my Aunt Margaret.

George and I are supposed to be sleeping. And tonight it is dark and cold and we could very well wrap ourselves in blankets and listen to the wind outside while the music billows below us. But sometimes it is still light out, and we smart under my mother's need to have us upstairs, disposed of for the night. We can hear the far voices of other children through the open screens, feel the cool breeze, imagine ourselves lying on our backs in the grass, looking up, wishing on the evening star. Or playing late in the growing dusk, *Annie-Annie-Over*, the call arcing over the garage roof long before the ball we know will follow.

Forty years, and summer sound brings it back. Warm weather in March—I should know enough to know you can't count on it—but listen: there is a whirring in the hedges beside the road that hints of crickets or frogs, the birds chatter as they settle in the bushes, and the open window of the car lets all the spring-time in. I might as well be eight. I might as well be wishing I could be outdoors when my mother has sent me to bed. I have the same deep longing to pick the voices apart, to lay them open and dissect what they are saying.

Sometimes I want so much to dance. But everyone is younger, or taller, or slimmer, and I know I would look foolish. Out of my time. I would look like someone who had always stood at the side while others danced, and I would feel stilted and a little stale. I want to be beautiful. Not beautiful in any way that you could recognize. I've given up on that. But I want to *feel* beautiful. Surely that could be possible. I have never been ugly—not the kind of ugly that knows itself for what it is and finds a way to cope. But I have been plain in a somewhat pleasant way. Plain enough to watch the men's eyes when other women enter the room. Plain enough to see to the root of things.

So this evening I switch off the car radio and the birds are making so much noise that it is argument and the warm air spills over my face and I wish I could be one of the women in long skirts sweeping through the doorway, unaware of the girl in pig-tails who lies dreaming at the top of the stairs. My life is so hur-ried. It has no evenings of soft chatter. No occasional riff of laugh-ter or spatter of heated opinion. No music to abandon itself to. It is full of whatever they shed as they walked through the door and let my mother take their coats.

Here is the movement of the mind: I am on my bicycle, pedal-ing no-handed under the whirling blades of maple seeds. Or run-ning up the steep hillside across the railroad tracks where we wear smooth trails pretending to be cowboys. Or playing with my doll house with its tiny shutters and its paper-doll world. Childhood reaches out its arms—I dance with it all night.

Even our cruelties are pure and passionate. *Ymyum, Ymyum,* Joanie Tubbs cries over and over as we stand before her. We have lifted her onto the trapeze and will not let her off until she can say our mother's name—Lillian. We love the way she struggles with the word. We love to see her squirm on her perch, like a trapped bird. Our hearts lift with pleasure as we shake our heads. How can we let her come down until she can make that sound? How can we let her into our childhood until she has suffered its rules?

March has broken all the rules. It shatters my complacent drive. I resist it. I know that tomorrow, and if not then, then the next day, the temperature will dip, the cold winds will blow in from Canada, the geese that wheel over me now will be a sign, but hardly significant. Spring is incremental here in upstate New York, and what I need is full-blown passion. Azaleas. A long walk through crowded streets. Lunch in the park. What I need is more than season can give me.

Snowdrops are ninety-nine percent snow. They rise from it, fade beneath its next onslaught. They come out in a brief spell of sun, as though to tempt us, barefoot, bereft. There is so much left behind. So little place to find it.

It's easier to feel beautiful on the telephone. The voice goes low, the laugh insinuates itself. You imagine he imagines you, and you imagine yourself in his imagination—taller, slimmer, less full of grief. The voice goes low and waits to catch its breath. You dance back and forth across the line, a tightrope stretched three stories up where summer never ends.

And if grief is your partner, then give it all you've got. It is tall, dark, and handsome. Its eyes blaze; it is angry, full of resentment. Dance with it. Wear white gloves and a corsage with two gardenias. You will catch its scent, lethal, and it will hold out to you the promise of everything you have ever lost. Your Aunt Margaret will dance into the room in woolen skirts from Guatemala. She will whirl and whirl and it will be your birthday. And then your Uncle Ray will lift you to the handlebars of his bicycle and take you to the tiny apartment in the brown-shingled house and you will believe you could stay there forever, reading your book in the fading light, someone else for a lifetime. Your mother will open the door and let loss in, in his black tuxedo, wearing his false face and kissing her fingers. He will betray every memory you have, but he will be a faithful lover.

155

I feel it all—the hop-and-skip of four years old, holding my father's hand to cross the road, the lonely night I held my son's three-week-old body on my shoulder and let The Beatles sing him to sleep, the car rolling through tonight's song of something on the verge of being. There is no present when the past pushes itself up out of the ground. Same color. Same spot. Same body, one year older. Same exact feeling, or feelings so exact that they resurface like snowdrops, spreading their frost on the lawn.

And why do I, watching, always feel as though I am watched?

What trick of memory stacks the past like cards in a pack? Shuffle, shuffle. Tap, tap. It is all the same. One life, reordered, served to order, sunny side up. See, here is the queen of diamonds, fate bound up in some dark man. Watch her thread her way through the pack, a waltz of red and gold. Whirl out with her and maybe you will forget your cares. She is Lucy in the Sky and Lucky D. She is everything you would have been if you had put on that skirt and come through the door. She is hair to her waist and wide collars. She is you on the wall—grown up.

Still, there is the dance that tugs and twitches. The Limbo. The place where you shuffle back and forth between imaginings. That is the place where you can't decide what you want or where you want to be. In it, life goes grey and drafty. It is neither a breeze nor a storm. Simply an annoyance. Grit in the eye. And somewhere the knowledge that seasons are turning without you.

In Brazil, full summer falls in January; sun hammers you, parched and shadowless, into the pavement. Every day the papers print statistics for drownings and dehydration. Death by water. Death by fire. You keep your children home from ten to three, playing quietly in the shade of the awning. Occasionally you take them into the *floresta* where trees seem visibly to grow and blue *morphos* glide silently from branch to branch slowly moving their wings, huge iridescent shapes that terrify more than they intrigue. The jungle writhes and chatters.

There are three dances in Brazil—or rather, three reasons for dancing. The first is old, as old as slavery. *Capoeira.* A ritual. A form of music and dance, of drumming and movement, rhythm embedded in rhythm, the bodies moving in intricate variations of stylized rage. Almost a fight—a dance to mask the fight—a dance to fool the masters so they do not recognize the martial art. The might. At night, you hear the drum change beat, and all the old rage sings.

February is the dance of Carnaval—a scarf of samba, a blur of manifest joy. This is the dream: for one night you will be rich and beautiful; you will dress like a queen; you will dance the night away; the sun will rise over your glistening shoulders. For one night, everyone is the same. This is the dream: you will leave your body; your life will stretch before you like someone else's future. You will see the Monday-morning sameness of your poverty. You will dance off in golden shoes, trailing a laugh. You will not look back.

The third is found in the courtyards of small back streets. On the corners of poor neighborhoods. At the beach on New Year's Eve. The hands on the drum move faster. The body itself becomes a drum, a syncopated candle in the sand. It moves and stutters, shudders with a final leap, the mouth opens to the pent-up sounds of whatever god has seized it. The body wrestles with its *orixá*; it speaks in tongues, twisting itself in a long, contorted dance of life.

This is not beauty. This frenzy is the stuff of faith, and its enervating aftermath. It is not available to me. It does not walk through the door and put its coat on a hanger. It does not check its hat. This is the shameless jungle growth, the jackfruit that splits on the ground with its scent of sperm. This is dried cod and passion fruit, the very taste of things beyond control. If there is innocence, it is not in the music, which intends to hold you in its spell. Intends to leave you filled and unfulfilled. A space where tense and voice are meaningless. Where language itself is spent. There are those of us who live inside the voice inside the head. We cannot leave ourselves behind. We do not move easily from seer to seen. This dance is not for us. We listen, but do not believe.

What we believe is the inner voice that proves to us that we exist. Mine is maddening. It will not speak in sentences. Hedges its bets with small disclaimers. Wears a sling for its broken collarbone. I listen to it, wanting more. Wanting to hear my own voice tell me that the woman driving home tonight *is* the child on the stairs and that soon, very soon, one sound will separate itself from all the rest. Aunt Margaret will clack her castanets and whirl and I will dance. I will become the song and the singer, escaping through the bannister into this moment when, although I should be sleeping, I am driving down an avenue of sound, beating my heavy blue wings, keeping awkward time on the dashboard while geese turn overhead, circling and circling in an impulse that somehow resembles a minuet.

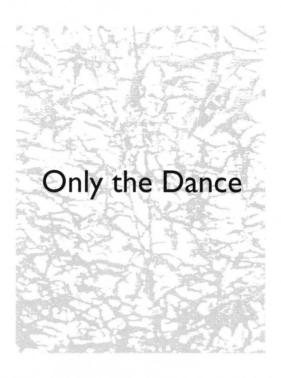

Only the Dance

October. Outside my window, purple flowers, pale as ghosts on tall, unwieldy stems. And by the fence, a flamboyance of late roses. Overnight, the trees have turned. Maples on fire. Or gone mottled, yellow to green to orange under our feet.

If only dying could be like this—a burst of flame, a final, triumphant shout to the silent universe: I was here, this is my blossoming, brief moment of consequence.

If only the body could rise, newly aware of itself, teeter on tentative legs and dance. Harvest of marrow. The body, so full of everything it never said, but, nevertheless, knew. And the knowledge, now, glistening in the late afternoon. Slant light. Granting a kind of dignity to the familiar. Soccer fields full of motion, young bodies spinning, the ball caught at the apex of its arc, everything shimmering and unreal. The upstairs windows of white frame houses remote in the sun's blank stare. Then the treeline, a fringe of black lace at the top of the hill, and the backdrop sky receding.

There's more to grief than this departure. Too many cycles. The trees are the color of daffodil, of tulip and iris and poppy. The eye does not stop reeling. And the body, slow burrowing creature, is afraid of its own shadow.

One life only. A bird's flight, blue flicker from branch to branch. And what do the bright pink roses on the fence know of frost? Of petals scattered like snowfall? "Death turns orange here," you say. The sumac flares.

Moors, Haworth, North Yorkshire

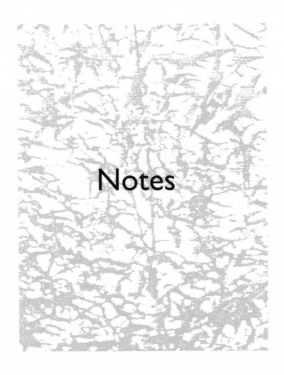

Notes

I consider this collection to be a reader's autobiography. Many of the essays are indebted to, or play against, the words of others. Rather than intrude on the immediate voice of the essay, I choose to cite some of my sources at the end of the book in the form of these notes. The information gathered for some of the essays set in the United Kingdom (especially in "Over the Sea To Skye") is taken from a variety of guidebooks and tourist pamphlets.

Hide-and-Go-Seek

The continuous sentence informing the essay is quoted from Tim O'Brien's *The Nuclear Age* (New York: Laurel Dell Publishing Co., 1985).

Robert Jimmy Allen

In 1992, I was asked by Sharon Bryan, editor of *River City*, to contribute to a "colloquium" on "women poets on literary tradition." She asked that we consider issues of gender in our relationship to poetry. In her introduction, she states, "I also asked if they thought they could have the same relationship to literary tradition as their male counterparts; if their responses to a male poet's work were affected by the way women appeared in those poems, and whether they were equally drawn to poems by men and by women. I pointed out the obvious, that teaching passes on attitudes toward literary tradition, and that publishing reflects and shapes those attitudes, and asked them to consider their own experiences in those areas. I asked if they had both women and men as poetry teachers, and if they thought it mattered." Bryan quoted from T. S. Eliot's "Tradition and the Individual Talent" and from Adrienne Rich. The women's collected essays were originally published in *River City*, Spring 1993, and then reprinted in *Where We Stand: Women Poets on Literary Tradition*, ed. Sharon Bryan (New York: W. W. Norton, 1993). In those publications, "Robert Jimmy Allen" appeared with the following postscript:

POSTSCRIPT

It would not take much of a deconstructionist to see the holes in my narrative, the places where I suspect I do protest too much. Or much of a feminist theorist to point the finger and say, Aha! Gender shapes us. It shaped me, I can see that. The culture is loud in its silence. Interestingly, through this silence, *because* of this silence, I taught myself to read—and then to write.

When I read, am I reading through the eyes of T. S. Eliot? Adrienne Rich says, "we need to know the writing of the past, and know it differently than we have ever known it, not to pass on a tradition but to break its hold over us." Am I, however inadvertently, passing on the tradition without changing it in the ways that Adrienne Rich insists we must? The answer is the old ambivalent "yes and no." But I am ambivalent about everything— about marriage and motherhood and writing and teaching, so why should this be any different? I feel responsibilities I don't want to feel.

The other day, an adjunct (female) in our English department asked of a newly hired feminist theorist (also female), "How do the feminists feel about Hawthorne?" I was terrified by the answer. Not by what she said (I've already forgotten that), but by the fact that she attempted to answer for all of us. She did not begin her sentence with, "I'm not sure what the 'feminists' think, but here's how I feel." *That* I would have understood. Because *that*, I always thought, was what we were fighting for.

Today, I spend much of my time reading books of poems, selecting from among stacks of new books the ones I will eventually review. In this capacity, I believe that I am helping to shape a tradition for the future. I am adding to it the voices of writers—male *and* female— whose words seem to me to deserve more readers. I must admit that I am aware of myself as a female reviewer. I admit that I feel (subtly) some pressure to be especially aware of the work of women and other minorities. I also admit that I may be hard on the work of women—if the images feel familiar (and they do, they do), then I want the writer to go beyond the *fact* of her femininity. I want to see the world through *her* eyes, not through some programmatic prescription. Such writing limits its possibilities in advance. If there is a "female" way of reading, it must be rooted in individual experience, individual imagination, ultimately in the individual body. And it must be accessible to other imaginations—potentially *all* others—as theirs must be to mine. If there is, indeed, something like a male tradition, then we need a female tradition which will be open to men, which will teach them to read as we do. I realize now that what I want is a wider tradition, not a different one. I don't want to set up the same old polarities, but to reconcile differences through understanding. This must be what the imagination is all about. Otherwise, why read? Why write? So I resist you, Adrienne Rich. I will not be pulled into your trap either. Because you, like Eliot, seem to be talking from *outside* the poem— and I want to come from inside. I want to be in that readerly place where gender is inconsequential.

Research

The epigraph is from Henri Bergson's *Matter and Memory*, translated by N. M. Paul and W. S. Palmer (New York: Zone Books, 1988). Other material is quoted from family letters, scrapbooks, and local newspapers.

Midge

Lines of poetry are quoted from *The Collected Poems of Sylvia Plath* (New York: Harper & Row, 1981). In sequential order they come from the following: "The Eye-Mote," 109; "Lady Lazarus," 244; "Stings," 214. Journal excerpts (appearing in italics) are quoted from *The Journals of Sylvia Plath* (New York: The Dial Press, 1982) appearing, in order, on pages 70, 259, 124, and 268. The individual song lyrics from the 1950s are taken from "Wayward Wind" sung by Gogi Grant, written by Stan Lebowsky and Herbert Newmann, copyright © 1955 PolyGram International Publishing, Inc. Used by permission. All rights reserved; "Oh! My Pa-pa" sung by Eddie Fisher, English words by John Turner and Geoffrey Parsons and music and original lyric by Paul Burkhard. Copyright © MCMLVIII, MCML Musicverlag und

Buhnenvertrieb Zurich A. G. Zurich, Switzerland. Copyright ©
MCMLIII Shapiro, Bernstein and Co., Inc. New York, New York.
All rights reserved. International copyright secured. Used by
permission.

Picnic at Paradise

The epigraph is from "Chicory" by William Stafford, *An Oregon Message* (New York: Harper & Row, 1987). The individual
lines of Stafford's poetry were taken from *Stories That Could Be
True: New and Collected Poems* (New York: Harper & Row, 1977)
and from *Passwords* (New York: Harper & Row, 1991). The poems quoted, in order, are "Ask Me," "Thinking for Berky," "Life
Work," "The Farm on the Great Plains," and, again, "Ask Me."
I also quote from Scott Russell Sanders' essay "Earth's Body," in
Staying Put (Boston: Beacon Press, 1993).

Not Less Because

Individual lines from Wallace Stevens appear in italics. They
were taken, almost at random, from *The Collected Poems of Wallace
Stevens* (New York: Random House, 1982).

White Roads

Passages from Leslie Norris appear in italics. In sequential
order, they come from the following: first three passages,
"Lurchers," *The Girl from Cardigan: Sixteen Stories* (Layton, UT:
Gibbs M. Smith, 1988) 119; "A House Divided," *Sliding* (New
York: Scribner, 1976) 60; "A Flight of Geese," *Girl*, 17; "The
Waxwings," *Sliding*, 4; "Sliding," *Sliding*, 11; "Early Frost," *Se-
lected Poems* (Brigend: Poetry Wales, 1986) 14; "A Roman Spring,"
Sliding, 134; "A Moonlight Gallop," *Sliding*, 107; "My Uncle's
Story," *Girl*, 41; "Sing it Again, Wordsworth," *Girl*, 24; "Prey,"
Sliding, 98.

Transitional

The English version of a Brazilian folk song (*cantiga de roda*) was translated by the author; the Portuguese words cited are from a contemporary samba, "Ella não gosta de mim," sung by Agepé on Brazil Classics 2 (*O Samba*), © 1989 Sire Records Company.

Songs to Undo the Spring

The epigraph is from "Burnt Norton" by T. S. Eliot, *Selected Poems, 1909–1935* (London: Faber & Faber).